A BEGINNER'S GUIDE TO
PRESERVING FOOD

Publications International, Ltd.

Let's get social!

 @Publications_International

 @PublicationsInternational

www.pilbooks.com

CHAPTER 1: COLD STORAGE AND DEHYDRATION.....................10

Canning: Before You Begin...................35

CHAPTER 2: PRINCIPLES OF HOME CANNING 38

CHAPTER 3: FERMENTED AND FRESH PICKLED VEGETABLES....76

CHAPTER 4: FRUIT AND FRUIT PRODUCTS 96

CHAPTER 5: JAMS AND JELLIES 136

CHAPTER 6: TOMATOES AND TOMATO PRODUCTS.............154

CHAPTER 7: VEGETABLES AND VEGETABLE PRODUCTS 176

COLD STORAGE AND DEHYDRATION

KEEPING IT COOL

Food preservation didn't begin with the 20th-century invention of refrigerators of course. Pre-refrigeration techniques included the use of root cellars, below-ground burial, cold pantries, drying and smoking techniques, and ice harvesting, to name a few. Long before refrigerators, people were air-drying sausages, burying crocks of meat underground, storing root vegetables in humidity- and temperature-controlled chambers, lining boxes with ice, and—high in the Andes—making the first freeze-dried mashed potatoes.

Chuno is the name for a type of freeze-dried potato developed by pre-Incan Andean cultures, dating back at least to the 12th century. In the high altitudes of the Andes, temperatures dip below freezing regularly. Local people made use of this fact by setting out potatoes to freeze overnight, which squeezed out the moisture. The process was repeated and the potatoes were then crushed underfoot. The resulting product could be stored with minimal care, remaining edible for a long time, sometimes decades.

While this method of food preservation may sound exotic to modern ears, we need only go back about four generations to discover a world of similarly sophisticated methods for keeping a variety of foods edible and free of pathogens. Food storage and preservation was a critical skill.

REFRIGERATOR STORAGE

Learning basic storage techniques will help keep your food fresh longer. A correctly working refrigerator should ensure that humidity levels, light, and temperature stay at optimal level. But you still need to set its controls for your needs and place food items properly. By learning to store things in proper areas, you will be able to ensure they don't go bad or become contaminated.

Refrigerated food should be kept at an optimal temperature of below 40 degrees Fahrenheit. This will inhibit the growth of bacteria.

A common mistake is overstuffing the refrigerator. When this happens, foods block the flow of air, making it harder for the refrigerator to maintain an even temperature. **Don't overstuff and don't push foods right up against the sides and back of the refrigerator** (as seen below). Try to keep everything separated by a half an inch.

Try to clean the refrigerator every three months to prevent the buildup of mold, mildew, and bacteria. This includes removing the trays and cleaning them with hot, soapy water. Consider using a solution of diluted bleach as well.

To keep the refrigerator smelling fresh, keep an open box of baking soda on a middle shelf.

Different areas of the refrigerator are best suited for different food items. The top shelves are the best place for leftovers, drinks, and herbs. Upper shelves typically have the most consistent temperature so they are a good place for foods that spoil easily. That said, the lower shelves are still going to be the best place to store dairy, raw meat, and eggs because this is the coldest area of the refrigerator. When storing leftovers, make sure to use airtight containers. This will prevent odors from getting out into the surrounding area. It's also a good idea to break up leftovers and store them in small containers. This cools leftovers more quickly, inhibiting the growth of bacteria.

Vegetables and fruits should be stored in the sealed drawers ("crispers"). Do not mix in meats with your fruits and vegetables as this can increase the risk of cross-contamination.

MEAT, FISH AND POULTRY

These are the items that need special care and vigilance, as they pose the greatest risk to your health. They should be placed in sealable containers so that no juices escape. They should always go in the coolest part of the refrigerator, usually near the bottom. Raw meat will go bad if not used in a few days, so store that in the freezer if it isn't going to be used immediately. Vacuum-sealed meat does not prolong the life of meat in a refrigerator.

COLD STORAGE DURATION

These guidelines will help you store food safely in your refrigerator. The time limits are short, but this ensures the items will not stay in the refrigerator long enough to spoil.

Food	Type	Refrigerate
Bacon and Sausage	Raw, from beef, chicken, pork, or beef	1 to 2 days
Beef, veal, lamb, and pork (fresh)	Chops	3 to 5 days
	Roasts	3 to 5 days
	Steaks	3 to 5 days
Eggs	Hard-cooked	1 week
	Raw in shell	3 to 5 weeks
Egg products	Casseroles with eggs	3 to 4 days
	Egg substitutes, frozen	Up to 1 week after thawing
	Egg substitutes, liquid	3 days after opening
	Eggnog, commercial	3 to 5 days
	Eggnog, homemade	2 to 4 days
	Pies, custard, chiffon, pecan, or pumpkin	3 to 4 days
	Quiche with filling	3 to 5 days

Food	Type	Refrigerate
Ham	Canned, shelf-stable, opened	5 to 14 days
	Cooked, wrapped at store, whole	1 week
	Cured, uncooked	5 to 7 days or "use by" date
	Cooked, wrapped at store, slices, half, or spiral cut	3 to 4 days
	Country ham, cooked	1 week
	Prosciutto, Parma, or Serrano, cut	2 to 3 months
Hot Dogs	Opened package	1 week
	Unopened package	2 weeks
Ground meat	Beef, lamb, pork, turkey, veal	1 to 2 days
Leftovers	Cooked meats, chicken nuggets, pizza	3 to 4 days
Lunch meat	Opened package or sliced deli meat	3 to 5 days
	Unopened package	2 weeks
Poultry	Fresh chicken or turkey, pieces	1 to 2 days
Salad	Chicken, egg, ham, macaroni, or tuna salads pieces	3 to 4 days
Soups and stews	Vegetable or meat added	3 to 4 days

FREEZER STORAGE

Most of us hardly notice the sheer convenience of having a freezer in the home. And in many cases, we don't realize that there are things we can do to keep frozen items in better condition, extending their life. Correct preparation and storage will help keep your frozen food in good shape. Knowing what freezes well is also key.

FOODS THAT FREEZE WELL

Bananas (peeled)	Meat (both raw and cooked)
Breads (sliced)	Nuts
Butter	Pasta (cooked, in sauce
Cakes and most baked goods	Rice (cooked, in sauce)
Some cheeses (grated)	Sausage
Flour	Stock

MEALS AND PREPARED FOODS THAT FREEZE WELL

Baby food	Fruit puree
Braised foods	Lasagna
Casseroles	Macaroni and cheese
Chili	Meatballs
Cookie dough	Pot pies
Curries	Soups and stews
Enchiladas	Tomato sauce

FREEZER BURN

Most of us know it when we taste it, but what is it? Freezer burn results from several factors. Primarily, it is the result of dehydration on the surface of frozen food. Before tasting it, you can visually spot it: discoloration or whitish splotches. And as moisture leaves, oxygen moves in. In the case of meat, the accelerated oxidation of fats results in a drier, tougher, off-tasting flavor.

To prevent freezer burn, you must **keep the water in and the oxygen out.** The ultimate solution is vacuum sealing, but most of us are unlikely to vacuum seal everything that goes into the freezer. Getting as much air out of your container is a good first step. When using a wrapping material, wrap your item as tightly as possible. Wax freezer paper and butcher paper are more effective than conventional plastic wrap. Double-wrapping helps too. Also consider rewrapping meat products that have been shrink-wrapped, for better protection. Cuts of meat can be dipped in water before wrapping. The added layer of moisture will be the first to evaporate, rather than the moisture within the item itself.

Another enemy is time: even the most carefully wrapped and sealed food will lose moisture over time. Try to cycle through your reserves to prevent your food from becoming too old. You can still eat freezer-burned food, but it does rob your food of nutritional value.

FOODS THAT DON'T FREEZE WELL

While freezing is a great option for extending the shelf life of some foods, not all foods freeze well. In some cases, this can be determined by water content. Foods with a high water content will suffer from separation. The food will still be edible, but the results will be disappointing. Keep in mind that being able to freeze food and getting an acceptable result after thawing is two different things.

Dairy, as a general rule, may acquire an undesirable texture as a result of freezing. The one exception to this is butter, which can be stored in the freezer for nine months. Most dishes with a high dairy content will not do well in the freezer.

The following foods do not freeze well. The list is not comprehensive; rather, these items are notorious for coming out of the freezer in poor condition.

- *Cakes with frosting will suffer weeping due to the egg content in the frosting.*
- *Cream cheese and sour cream separates and becomes lumpy when thawed.*
- *Custards and meringues suffer weeping and separation.*
- *Dishes with cheese or crumb toppings lose crispiness and become soggy after defrosting.*
- *Egg whites suffer from freezing, becoming soft, spongy, or rubbery.*
- *Fried food will lose its crispy coating after defrosting, becoming mushy.*
- *Fruits like apples, grapefruit, grapes, lemons, limes, oranges, and watermelon do not freeze well.*

- *Gravy and sauces will separate.*

- *Jellies and gelatin will weep, becoming a liquid mess when thawed.*

- *Mayonnaise separates.*

- *Milk does not freeze well because the fat separates from the liquid, becoming lumpy when thawed.*

- *Pasta loses its shape and texture when stored by itself. It does better when frozen in a sauce.*

- *Shellfish may be frozen before cooking. Once it's cooked, it should not be refrozen.*

- *Some spices will change their flavor when frozen. Be aware that pepper, cloves, and imitation vanilla tend to get strong and bitter.*

- *Vegetables that do not freeze well on their own include cabbage, celery, cress, cucumbers, some herbs, Irish potatoes, onions, peppers (especially green), radishes, most salad greens, sprouts, tomatoes, and zucchini.*

- *Yogurt separates and can develop an acidic taste.*

The fruits in this list are high in water content. But preparation after thawing is key here; if you're just going to blend the fruit into a recipe like a smoothie, the texture won't be as important.

FREEZER STORAGE DURATION

The general rule is to keep things in the freezer no longer than nine months to a year. But there is variation amongst different food items. Here are some rough guidelines to how long you can keep specific foods frozen before thawing.

Food	Type	Freeze up to
Bacon and sausage	Bacon	1 month
	Raw or cooked sausage from beef, chicken, pork, or turkey	2 months
Beef, veal, lamb, pork, and wild game (fresh)	Chops, roasts, steaks	1 year
Bread and cake	Cooked	6 months
	Dough	3 months
Cookies	Baked	3 months
	Dough	2 months
Dairy	Most cheeses	6 months
	Ice cream	4 months
	Salted butter	4 months
	Unsalted butter	8 months
Fish	Clams, mussels, oysters, or shrimp	6 months
	White fish	8 months
	Oily fish	4 months
Fruit	In syrup	1 year
	Juice	8 months
	Open packs of frozen fruit	8 months
Ground meat	Beef, lamb, pork, turkey, veal	4 months

Food	Type	Freeze up to
Ham	Fresh, uncured, cooked or uncooked	6 months
	Cooked, wrapped at store, whole	2 months
	Cured, uncooked	4 months
	Cooked, wrapped at store, slices, half, or spiral cut	2 months
	Country ham, cooked	1 month
	Prosciutto, Parma, or Serrano, cut	1 month
Hot dogs		2 months
Leftovers	Casseroles	3 months
	Chicken nuggets or patties	3 months
	Cooked meat or poultry	6 months
	Pizza	2 months
Lunch meat		2 months
Pastries		4 months
Pies	Fruit, baked	4 months
	Fruit, unbaked	8 months
	Pumpkin or chiffon	1 month
Poultry	Chicken or turkey, pieces	9 months
	Chicken or turkey, whole	1 year
Sauces, soups, and stews		3 months
Vegetables	Blanched	1 year

DO'S, DON'TS, AND TIPS

Don't refreeze raw food. Freezing doesn't kill all pathogens. Once you thaw the food, the more resilient microorganisms present in the food can revive and multiply quickly. Refreezing can mean much higher levels of microbes the second time around.

Separate the portions meant for freezing before you serve the dish at the table. This keeps the food quality higher (it hasn't been picked over) and keeps the food safer.

Cool your food before freezing. You don't want to introduce hot foods into a freezer where they can raise the ambient temperature for a while, possibly defrosting the surrounding foods. Instead, cool the food first. Try to place food in a shallow container on a cooling rack so that cool air can circulate around it.

Freeze food quickly. What you take out of the freezer is only as good as what goes in. It's best to freeze food when it's at its freshest.

Choose appropriate packaging. Freezer air is very dry. When food stored in the freezer is exposed to this air, it loses moisture, acquires freezer burn, and ends up tasting bad. Choose airtight freezer-appropriate plastic bags and containers.

Freeze food in small portions. This allows you to only defrost what you need. Freezing small portions also means shorter defrost times.

Label your freezer foods so that next time you pull something out of the freezer, you know what it is and when it was frozen. Write the name of the food, when it was packaged, and the number of servings in the package.

FREEZING HERBS

Storing fresh herbs in the freezer can save you money and prevent wastage. A little bit of knowledge and preparation will help ensure that what you pull out of the freezer is as fresh and pungent as possible.

Make sure your herbs are clean. Give fresh herbs a good wash in cool water and then pat them dry.

Put them in the freezer briefly. Spread the herbs out on a tray and leave them in the freezer for up to an hour.

Put herbs in a sealed container. Add the herbs to your container and try to push as much air out as possible. Label your containers with the name of the herb and the date frozen. Plastic freezer bags work best.

DEHYDRATION

An ancient method of food preservation, dehydration is both convenient and sophisticated. It's a time-tested method that requires little more than the sun, though it can also be accomplished more quickly (and expensively) with ovens or electric dehydrators.

Dehydrated food is an increasingly popular sight. It's hard to miss: aisles of dried, shriveled fruit (think banana chips, apple rings, and orange peels) populate many of our favorite grocery stores. This food is easy to transport, lightweight, and is a fantastic (and healthy) snacking option.

However, there are some potential downsides to dehydration. For one, dried foods can lose too much moisture, which can make them lacking in nutrients like vitamins A and C and thiamin. They can carry more calories on a weight-for-weight basis than non-dried food. And their textures can rapidly change, making them difficult to consume, tough on your teeth, and be off-putting to those with sensitive taste buds. Indeed, some see them as an acquired taste.

Despite some downsides, dried foods are indisputably healthy, and dehydration can be accomplished with little more than a heat source and time.

DEHYDRATION'S HISTORY

Historians say dehydration wasn't an invention; rather, it was a discovery. Thousands of years ago, Egyptians used the sun to heat and dry fish and other food animals. Thousands of years later, medieval Europeans created *still houses* to dry fruits, vegetables, and herbs, in some cases smoking them as well.

In the nineteenth century, French inventors developed a process known as mechanized dehydration. Vegetables were dried with 105-degree air and then compressed into cakes.

In America, dehydration's popularity waxed and waned throughout the nineteenth and twentieth centuries. Rations during World War II boosted its popularity, for dried foods proved to be a lightweight alternative to other foodstuffs. Dehydration's appeal surged throughout the second half of the century, as campers grew enthralled by this lightweight and transportable preservation technique. In recent years, dehydration has become increasingly trendy.

DEHYDRATION METHODS

How does one go about drying food? Consider these three basic avenues:

Solar Drying: Similar to sun drying, solar drying utilizes the sun's rays to remove moist air from a dehydrating unit. Solar drying features a shorter drying time than regular sunlight because the unit is warmer than regular sunlight.

Oven Drying: Oven drying is a popular method for dehydration. Ovens help protect food from pests and inclement weather. However, they are less energy efficient than electric dehydrators, and oven-dried food is considered less flavorful than other methods.

Electric Drying: An electric dehydrator is considered the most effective (and most expensive) way of drying. A self-contained electric dehydrator features a ventilation system and heat source, which allows for easy indoor drying. They don't rely on the sun, aren't at the mercy of poor weather, and require little energy.

Of course, shelling out excessive dollars for an oven or electric dryer isn't always an option. But once you become more experienced, they may become increasingly attractive.

There are a number of things to consider before purchasing a dehydrator. And before considering any of them, experiment with an oven to get the hang of the process.

When you're ready, consider the following:

Space: Electric dehydrators come in different sizes and shapes; the key is to find a smart spot to operate the machine. And don't forget that food gives off plenty of humidity, and the dehydrator gives off heat and makes noise.

Air flow: Warm, dry air is essential to the dehydration process. Most dryers use a fan, while others utilize convection. In general, fans boost air circulation; a high speed fan helps early in the drying process, and a low speed fan is used later to remove excess moisture.

Trays: Trays should slide in and out, allow for plenty of circulation, and be high enough to prevent food from spilling or falling. They should also be lightweight.

Door: The machine's door should have a strong seal, solid hinges, and be easy to open and close. Its latches should be able to endure heat.

DEHYDRATION WITHOUT A DEHYDRATOR

Before you consider looking at dehydrators (which typically cost, at most, a couple of hundred dollars), experiment with the following:

Using the sun. This is an easy and inexpensive way to get the job done. You'll need three to four days of direct sunlight and low humidity levels; a humidity level below 25 percent is most ideal. However, attempting this method in many climates may not be feasible, as moist and cool air can quickly promote mold growth.

Drying indoors. Many mushrooms and herbs can be dried indoors. Simply tie the food on a string and hang them (if you're noticing similarities to the still houses of medieval times, you're right). You can place the produce in a paper bag, or something similar, to prevent dust or other household contamination.

Using the oven. A more modern method is the oven. Preheat the oven to 140 degrees Fahrenheit and keep the oven door slightly ajar. Put the food on a baking sheet. Herbs will dry in little more than an hour, but thicker foods like peaches could take up to two days.

BEFORE DEYHYDRATION

Certain foods (like peaches, apples, and apricots) need sulfur applications to ward off browning. While a sulfur treatment may destroy thiamin, the treatment should protect vitamins A and C and prevent the loss of flavor. Consider these two options:

Sulfuring: Sulfuring is used primarily on sun-dried fruits; sulfured fruits cannot be dried inside, as sulfur fumes can irritate the eyes, skin, and mucous membranes. Few nutrients are removed during this treatment, which makes sulfuring incredibly effective; however, this option is also very expensive and time-consuming to complete.

Sulfiting: Unlike sulfuring, sulfite-dipped foods can easily absorb water (meaning longer drying times) and lose nutrients more quickly than sulfuring. Nevertheless, sulfite dips are easy to prepare and can be dried indoors.

Sulfiting requires the following steps:

- *Dissolve no more than 1½ teaspoons of sodium bisulfate (or no more than 3 teaspoons of sodium sulfite) per quart of water.*

- *Place the fruit in the mixture and soak slices for up to five minutes. Fruit halves can soak for up to 15 minutes.*

- *Remove the fruit and rinse it under cold water.*

- *Place the fruit on drying trays.*

BLANCHING

The purpose of blanching is simple: to stop the cooking process. To blanch is to temporarily scald food in hot water. Blanching, performed alongside a sulfite pretreatment, can delay the loss of nutrients.

Steam blanching: Steam blanching can alter a food's texture and flavor, but helps retain color and slow oxidation. To steam blanch, perform the following steps:

1. Place about 2 inches of water in a large pot with a lid. Heat pot to boiling.

2. Place fruit in a steamer pan or wire basket over the boiling water. Cover with lid, and begin timing. Most fruits take no more than five minutes to blanch.

3. After the blanch is complete, remove leftover moisture with paper towels. Place blanched food on dryer trays.

Syrup blanching: Syrup blanching makes a product similar to candied fruit and helps keep food color. Many fruits can be blanched with this method, including apples, figs, plums, prunes, peaches, and apricots.

To syrup blanch, perform the following steps:

1. Combine 1 cup corn syrup, 1 cup sugar, and 2 cups water in a pot and bring to boil.

2. Add 1 pound prepared fruit and simmer for about 10 minutes.

3. Remove from heat and let stand in syrup for about 30 minutes.

4. Remove fruit from syrup and rinse in cold water.

5. Place fruit on dryer racks.

Like fruits, the amount of time it takes to blanch a vegetable varies depending on its thickness. Blanching vegetables puts the brakes on enzyme activity, which in turn prevents browning and off-putting flavor change. The process also protects vegetables from nutrient loss and spoilage.

CHECKING

Some foods (such as grapes and cherries) that are dried need to be "checked" to crack their skins and remove their coatings. Checking allows moisture to quickly evaporate and helps accelerate drying. To check foods, immerse them in boiling water for no more than 60 seconds and then quickly place them in cold water. This process can also be completed in a microwave: simply heat the food on high for no more than 30 seconds and then place in cold water.

DRYING FRUITS IN A DEHYDRATOR

Follow these simple steps to dry your favorite fruits.

Wash the fruit. This is an optional step, but it is a generally healthy idea.

Peel the fruit if it isn't edible. Fruit normally consumed without peeling can be consumed in this state when dried.

Slice the fruit. Larger fruits should be sliced into pieces no greater than one half-inch. Smaller fruits do not need to be sliced or halved.

Place slices on a single layer. Keep the slices far enough apart so that they will not stick together (the edges can touch but should not overlap).

Set the correct time and temperature. This will vary depending on what the dehydrator's manual recommends. If there is no manual or directions, set the temperature between 120 and 140 degrees Fahrenheit. A lower temperature will result in more consistently dry fruit, and a higher temperature will expedite the process.

Let fruit cool. The dried fruit should be ready to eat anywhere from six to more than 24 hours. A multitude of factors--including your dehydrator's power, the air's humidity, and size and type of fruit--will determine the timetable.

Store fruit. Fruit that will be consumed in less than 30 days can be stored in resealable jars, plastic storage containers, or bags. If you're planning on storing the fruit for months, consider a vacuum sealer.

DRY, OR NOT DRY?

For dehydration newcomers, it can be difficult to tell when food is thoroughly dry. As a rule of thumb, it's better to overdry than underdry.

Vegetables should be brittle and have sharp edges. They should have a leathery texture.

There should be no moisture from **fruits** following the drying process. They should be tough and challenging to cut.

Outside of long-term storage or refrigeration, **meats** should always appear thoroughly dry. Visible clues include dark-colors and sharp points.

Herbs are simple: If they are brittle, then they are dry. Rub their leaves together; they should fall apart.

CONDITIONING AND PASTEURIZING

In most circumstances, conditioning and pasteurizing should be completed before storing dried food.

Conditioning: Conditioning involves equalizing leftover moisture after drying. It is done to prevent mold or other spoilages from taking place. The process requires the following steps:

- *Cool all food from trays.*
- *Pour food into a large container and fill about half-full.*
- *Cover the container and place in a dry place.*
- *Check for any signs of mold or other spoilages. If condensation is present, place food back in the dryer.*
- *Cool, then package.*

Pasteurizing: Pasteurizing is a good way to deal with contamination. This method helps food that is currently spoilage-free. The process can be completed by way of two methods:

Oven: Put food in a single layer on a tray. Transfer tray to an oven that is set to 160 degrees Fahrenheit for 30 minutes. Remove the tray from the oven and package the food for storage.

Freezer: Seal dried food in a plastic bag. Place in a freezer at zero degrees for about three days.

PACKAGING AND STORING TIPS

Consider these tips for packaging and storing dried food:

- **Store foods in cool, dry, and dark places. Cellars and basements are popular choices.**

- **Keep dried foods in airtight containers.**

- **Package food in small amounts to prevent moisture from entering containers.**

- **Store foods in temperatures under 60 degrees Fahrenheit. Foods stored in temperatures above 60 degrees will deteriorate in under one year.**

CANNING: BEFORE YOU BEGIN

The next section provides instructions for preparing fruits and vegetables for canning, making pickles with and without fermentation, and processing jars of home-canned foods with boiling-water canners and pressure canners, all in accordance with current guidelines established by the U.S. Department of Agriculture (USDA).

Ongoing research often affects recommendations for home food preservation. Make sure you always use up-to-date, tested guidelines.

FOR SAFETY'S SAKE

Clostridium botulinum bacteria are the culprits behind a potentially deadly form of food poisoning called botulism. If these bacteria survive and grow inside a sealed jar of food, they can produce the poisonous botulinum toxin. Just tasting food containing this toxin can be fatal.

Clostridium botulinum bacteria are destroyed in low-acid foods when those foods are processed at the correct pressure and for the correct amount of time in a pressure canner. Using a boiling-water canner instead poses a risk of botulism poisoning. (We will cover botulism later). Pressure canning is the only recommended method for canning vegetables. To avoid any risk of botulism, always follow the procedures in this guide, or in publications endorsed by the USDA, in canning low-acid or tomato-based foods.

If you're using home-canned tomatoes or low-acid food that may have been prepared with any deviation from USDA methods, you should boil the food in a pan before serving it, **even if you detect no signs of spoilage.** At an altitude of 1,000 feet or below, boil the questionable food for 10 minutes. At a higher altitude, add another minute of boiling time for each 1,000 feet of elevation. If you know that the food has been significantly underprocessed according to current USDA standards, you shouldn't use it at all.

You can safely forgo boiling home-canned tomatoes and low-acid foods if you're sure that:

- *The food was processed in a pressure canner.*

- *The canner had an accurate pressure gauge.*

- *Up-to-date recommendations were followed for process time and pressure.*

- *The time and pressure were correct for the size of jar, the kind of food, the way it was packed, and your altitude.*

- *The jar lid has remained firmly sealed and concave.*

- *Nothing has leaked from the jar.*

- *No liquid spurts out when the jar is opened.*

- *You detect no strange odors.*

DO YOUR CANNED FOODS PASS THIS TEST?

To evaluate foods that you have canned yourself at home, check to see if the following are true:

OVERALL APPEARANCE

- *Good proportion of solids to liquid*

- *Proper headspace*

- *Liquid just covers the solids*

- *No air bubbles*

- *No stems, cores, or seeds*

- *Good seals*

- *Quick and easy process*

LIQUID OR SYRUP

- *Clear and free of sediment*

FRUIT AND VEGETABLES

- *Proper maturity*

- *Uniformly sized and shaped pieces*

- *Retained shape—no broken or mushy pieces*

- *Good, uniform color*

DETERMINING YOUR ALTITUDE ABOVE SEA LEVEL

Since the boiling temperature of liquid is lower at higher elevations, foods must be processed longer at higher altitudes. It is important to know your approximate altitude, or elevation above sea level, to determine safe processing times for the foods you can. Kansas isn't considered a mountainous state, but altitudes there range from 75 feet to 4,039 feet above sea level. Home-canners in Colorado are generally aware of the need to make altitude adjustments, and yet the needed adjustments there vary, for elevations from 3,000 feet to 10,000 feet above sea level.

Because altitudes can vary widely within a particular state or even county, it would be impractical to include a list of altitudes in this guide. If you are unsure about the altitude where you live (or where you do your canning), consult your county Cooperative Extension agent or a local representative of the Natural Resources Conservation Service.

PRINCIPLES OF HOME CANNING

WHY CAN FOODS?

Canning can be a safe and economical way to preserve food at home. Leaving out the value of your labor, canning homegrown food may save you half the cost of buying commercially canned food. Added to this savings is the pleasure you'll take in sharing your own special canned foods with your family and friends.

If fruits and vegetables are handled properly and canned promptly after harvest, they can actually be more nutritious than fresh produce sold in local stores. Many fruits and vegetables begin losing some of their vitamins as soon as they're harvested. In fact, nearly half the vitamins may be lost within a few days unless the fresh produce is refrigerated or preserved. Within 1 to 2 weeks, even refrigerated produce loses half or more of some vitamins. In the canning process, heat destroys from a third to half of vitamins A and C, thiamin, and riboflavin. Once the produce is canned, additional losses of these vitamins are from 5 to 20 percent each year. But the amounts of other vitamins are only slightly lower in canned compared with freshly harvested produce.

The advantages of home canning are lost, however, if you start with subpar produce; if your jars fail to seal; if food spoils in the jars for some reason; or if you keep the jars on the shelf so long that flavor, texture, color, and nutrients deteriorate. The text that follows explains many of these problems and recommends ways to minimize or avoid them.

HOW CANNING PRESERVES FOODS

The high percentage of water in most fresh foods makes them very perishable. They spoil or lose their quality for several reasons:

- *The growth of undesirable microorganisms (bacteria, molds, and yeasts)*

- *The activity of food enzymes*

- *Reactions with oxygen*

- *Moisture loss*

Microorganisms live and multiply quickly on the surfaces of fresh fruits and vegetables. If the produce is bruised, insect-damaged, or diseased, microbes can multiply on the inside, too. And oxygen and enzymes are present throughout the insides of fresh foods.

Proper canning practices are designed to mitigate these factors and protect preserved foods from spoilage and loss of quality. These practices include:

- *Carefully selecting and washing fresh foods*

- *Peeling fresh fruits and vegetables when appropriate*

- *Heating foods before packing them when appropriate*
- *Adding acid (lemon juice or vinegar) to some foods*
- *Using canning jars with self-sealing lids*
- *Processing jars in a boiling-water or pressure canner for the right amount of time*

Collectively, these practices remove oxygen from the jars; destroy enzymes; prevent the growth of undesirable bacteria, yeasts, and molds; and help form a strong vacuum. A strong vacuum forms a tight seal that keeps liquid in and air and microorganisms out.

ENSURING SAFE CANNED FOODS

Growth of the bacterium *Clostridium botulinum* in canned food can cause botulism—a deadly form of food poisoning. Botulinum bacteria exist as either spores or vegetative cells. The spores, which are comparable to plant seeds, can survive in soil and water for many years without doing any harm. But when exposed to ideal conditions for growth, the spores produce vegetative cells, which multiply rapidly. These cells can produce a deadly toxin within 3 to 4 days of growth if they're in an environment consisting of:

- *Moist food that has a low acid content*
- *A temperature that falls between 40 degrees and 120 degrees Fahrenheit (°F)*
- *Less than 2 percent oxygen*

Botulinum spores are present on the outer surfaces of most fresh foods. Because these spores grow only in the absence of air, they are normally harmless. A sealed canning jar, however, can provide ideal conditions for these spores to start producing vegetative cells.

Like other bacteria, yeasts, and molds, botulinum spores are quite difficult to remove from food surfaces. Washing the produce reduces spore counts only slightly. Peeling tomatoes and vegetables that grow underground greatly reduces the numbers of botulinum spores. Blanching also helps. When you're canning vegetables, though, the best way to destroy the spores is by using the methods and processing times specified in this guide.

The way you store your filled jars is important, too. Assuming you process the jars correctly and the lids all seal tightly, your home-canned foods won't spoil as long as you store them at a temperature below 95°F. But to keep your canned foods at their best for the greatest period of time, you should store the jars at 50° to 70°F.

FOOD ACIDITY AND PROCESSING METHODS

Whether food should be processed in a pressure canner or a boiling-water canner to control botulinum bacteria depends on the acidity of the food. Acid may be naturally present in a food, as is the case with most fruits, or added, as in pickled foods. **Low-acid foods** are those that aren't acidic enough to prevent the growth of these bacteria. **Acid foods** contain enough acid to block the growth of botulinum bacteria or destroy them rapidly with heating. The acidity level of foods can be increased by adding lemon juice, citric acid, or vinegar.

The term **pH** refers to a measure of acidity; the lower the pH of a food, the more acidic it is. Low-acid foods, on the other hand, have pH values higher than 4.6. These foods include red meats, seafood, poultry, milk, and all fresh vegetables except for most tomatoes. Most mixtures of low-acid and acid foods also have pH values above 4.6, unless the recipes include plenty of lemon juice, citric acid, or vinegar.

Acid foods have a pH of 4.6 or lower. They include fruits (except figs), pickles, sauerkraut, jams, jellies, marmalades, and fruit butters. Acid foods can be processed safely in a boiling-water canner.

Although tomatoes are usually considered an acid food, some varieties have pH values slightly above 4.6. Figs also have pH values slightly above 4.6. So if you want to can figs or low-acid tomatoes as acid foods, you must add lemon juice or citric acid. Properly acidified tomatoes and figs can be safely processed the same way as other fruits—in a boiling-water canner.

The time needed to process acid foods in a boiling-water canner varies from 5 to 85 minutes. The exact time depends on the kind of food being canned, the way it is packed into jars, and the jar size.

Because botulinum spores are very hard to destroy at the temperature of boiling water unless there is sufficient acid present, low-acid foods should be processed at a higher temperature, between 240° and 250°F. This temperature range can be attained with a pressure canner operated at 10 to 15 **pounds per square inch (PSI)** of pressure as measured by a gauge. At 240° to 250°F, the time needed to destroy bacteria in low-acid canned food ranges from 20 to 100 minutes. Safely processing low-acid foods in a boiling-water canner, on the other hand, would take much longer, from 7 to 11 hours.

ADJUSTING FOR HIGH ALTITUDES

Using the processing time specified for canning food at sea level could result in spoilage if you live (and do your canning) at an altitude above 1,000 feet. This is because water boils at lower temperatures as altitude increases, and lower boiling temperatures are less effective at killing bacteria. To compensate for the lower boiling temperature at a higher elevation, you need to increase the processing time or canner pressure. The recipes in this guide provide appropriate processing times and canner pressures for sea-level canning and for canning at higher elevations. So when using one of these recipes, select the processing time or canner pressure listed for the altitude where you live. If you don't know the altitude of your home, ask your county Cooperative Extension agent or a local representative of the Natural Resources Conservation Service, formerly known as the Soil Conservation Service. (See the box on page 47 for more information about these resources and how to contact them.)

EQUIPMENT AND METHODS THAT AREN'T RECOMMENDED

Even with acidic foods, "open-kettle canning"—that is, filling hot jars with hot food, sealing the jars, and skipping the processing step—doesn't prevent all risk of spoilage. Nor does processing jars in a microwave, conventional oven, or dishwasher. The U.S. Department of Agriculture (USDA) doesn't recommend steam canners, either, although they are widely available, because not enough research has been done into proper and safe processing times for use with current models.

So-called canning powders are useless as preservatives and So-called canning powders are useless as preservatives and do not replace the need for proper heat processing.

Antique mason jars with wire bails and glass caps make attractive storage containers for dry foods, but they are no longer recommended for use in canning. Nor are one-piece zinc caps lined with porcelain. The rubber rings used with both glass and zinc caps too often fail to seal properly. Finally, when using a new pressure canner, avoid applying pressure in excess of 15 PSI.

ENSURING HIGH-QUALITY CANNED FOODS

Begin with good fresh produce. Apricots, nectarines, peaches, pears, and plums may need to be ripened for a day or longer between harvest and canning. If you must delay the canning of other fresh produce, keep it in a shady, cool place. Most vegetables are at their peak of quality for only 6 to 12 hours after harvest.

Discard any vegetables or fruits that appear diseased or moldy. Trim off any small spots of disease or injury.

Some vegetable or fruit varieties may be better suited for canning than others. If you need recommendations, consult your county Cooperative Extension office (see the box on the following page).

MAINTAINING COLOR AND FLAVOR IN CANNED FOODS

To maintain good natural color and flavor in stored canned food, you must:

- *Remove oxygen from the food tissues and from the jars*

- *Quickly destroy the enzymes in the food*

- *Attain strong vacuums in the jars and airtight seals*

To ensure that your canned food retains its optimum color and flavor during both processing and storage, follow these guidelines:

- *Use only foods that are at the proper maturity and free of diseases and bruises.*

- *Use the hot-pack method, especially with acid foods that you'll be processing in a boiling-water canner.*

- *Avoid unnecessarily exposing prepared food to air. As soon as you have prepared food for canning, put it into jars and process the jars.*

- *While you are peeling and cutting apples, apricots, nectarines, peaches, or pears for canning, keep the cut fruit in a solution of 3 grams (3,000 milligrams) of ascorbic acid to 1 gallon of cold water. This technique can also help to preserve the natural color of potatoes and prevent discoloration of the stem end of cherries and grapes.*

- *Allow no more or less headspace in the jar than is specified in the recipe.*

- *Tighten screw bands securely but, if you are especially strong, not as tightly as possible.*

- *Store your processed and cooled jars in a place that's dark and cool (preferably between 50° and 70°F).*

- *Can no more food than you will use within a year.*

BUYING ASCORBIC ACID

You can get ascorbic acid in several forms:

- *Pure powdered ascorbic acid is seasonally available among canners' supplies in supermarkets. Use 1 level teaspoon (about 3 grams) of the powder as a treatment solution.*

- *Vitamin C tablets are inexpensive and easy to find year-round. Crush and dissolve six 500-milligram tablets per gallon of water.*

- *Commercially prepared mixes of ascorbic and citric acid are available in supermarkets during canning season. Follow the manufacturer's directions if you're using one of these combination products. (Citric-acid powder alone is also sometimes available, but it is less effective against discoloration.)*

RAW-PACKING VERSUS HOT-PACKING

Many fresh foods contain from 10 to more than 30 percent air. How long canned food retains its high quality depends on how much air is removed from the food before the jars are sealed.

Raw-packing is the practice of filling jars tightly with freshly prepared but unheated food. Such food, especially fruit, will tend to float in the jars. Air trapped in and around the food may cause discoloration within 2 to 3 months of storage. Raw-packing is most suitable for vegetables processed in a pressure canner.

Hot-packing is the practice of heating freshly prepared food to boiling, simmering it for 2 to 5 minutes, and promptly filling jars loosely with the boiled food. Hot-packing is the best way to remove air and usually the preferred way to pack foods that will be processed in a boiling-water canner. At first, the color of hot-packed foods may appear no better than that of raw-packed foods, but after a short period of storage, both the color and flavor of hot-packed foods will be superior.

Whether you're hot-packing or raw-packing, the juice, syrup, or water that you're adding to the jars should be heated to boiling first. This will help to remove air from the food tissues, keep the food from floating, increase the vacuum, and improve the shelf life of your canned food. The hot liquid will also quickly shrink the solid pieces, allowing you to fit more into each jar.

CONTROLLING HEADSPACE

The empty space between the food in a jar and the jar lid is called headspace. This space allows for the expansion of the food as the jars are processed and the formation of a vacuum as the jars cool. How much a food expands during processing depends on its air content and the processing temperature; the higher the temperature and the greater the air content, the more the food will expand. Jams and jellies need ¼ inch headspace; fruits and tomatoes to be processed in a boiling-water canner need ½ inch; and low-acid foods to be processed in a pressure canner need 1 to 1¼ inches.

JARS AND LIDS

Food can be canned in glass jars or metal containers. Metal containers can be used only once. They require special sealing equipment and are much more costly than jars.

Regular and wide-mouth Mason jars with self-sealing lids and metal screw bands are the best choice for most home canners. A regular jar has an opening of $2\frac{3}{8}$ inches in diameter; a wide-mouth jar has an opening of about 3 inches. Both types of jars are available in half-pint (8-ounce), pint (16-ounce), 1½-pint (24-ounce), quart (32-ounce), and half-gallon (64-ounce) sizes. Wide-mouth jars are easier to fill and empty if the food you are canning is in large pieces. Regular-mouth, decorative jelly jars are available in 8- and 12-ounce sizes. Half-gallon jars can be used for canning very acid juices. With careful use and handling, Mason jars can be reused many times.

Most commercial pint- and quart-size mayonnaise or salad-dressing jars can be reused for canning acid foods in a boiling-water canner as long as you seal them with new 2-piece Mason caps (caps consisting of a self-sealing flat lid and a metal screw band). But you should expect more seal failures and glass breakage with these jars, which have narrower rims and are less tempered than Mason jars. Repeated contact with metal spoons or knives may have weakened a jar that once held mayonnaise. Seemingly insignificant scratches in the glass could cause cracking and breakage during processing.

Mayonnaise jars are not recommended for use in a pressure canner, where they would tend to break.

Commercial jars with mouths that won't accommodate 2-piece Mason caps are not recommended for home canning regardless of the method used.

CLEANING AND PREHEATING JARS

Immediately before every use, wash empty jars in hot water with detergent, rinse the jars well, and keep them hot until you're ready to fill them. Using a dishwasher and leaving it closed after the cycle has finished is an easy way to keep jars hot until you need them. If you wash your jars by hand instead, submerge them in simmering water (at 180°F) in a large stockpot or boiling-water canner until you are ready to fill them.

STERILIZING EMPTY JARS

All jams, jellies, and pickled foods that will be processed for less than 10 minutes should go in sterile jars. Sterilizing is different than preheating. To sterilize jars: After washing them in detergent and rinsing them thoroughly, place them right-side up in a boiling-water canner with a rack in the bottom. Fill the canner with warm water to 1 inch above the tops of the jars. Bring the water to a boil, and boil for 10 minutes if your altitude is no greater than 1,000 feet. At a higher elevation, boil for an additional minute for each 1,000 feet above sea level. When the jars have boiled long enough, reduce the heat under the canner, and keep the jars in the hot water until it is time to fill them. Remove, drain, and fill the jars one at a time. Return the filled, capped jars to the canner for processing.

If you will be processing jars in a pressure canner, you need not sterilize them first. Nor do you need to sterilize jars that will be processed for at least 10 minutes in a boiling-water canner.

> ### TIP
> You may notice a white film on the outsides of some used Mason jars. Called **scale,** this film is caused by mineral deposits. You can easily remove it by soaking the jars for several hours in a solution of 1 cup vinegar (5 percent acidity) to 1 gallon water.

SELECTING AND USING JAR LIDS AND BANDS

The common self-sealing Mason jar cap consists of a flat metal lid held in place during processing by a metal screw band. The flat lid is crimped at its edge to form a trough on the underside, and the trough is filled with sealing compound to form a gasket. When a jar is processed, this gasket softens and flows slightly to cover the rim yet allows air to escape the jar. As the jar cools, the gasket forms an airtight seal. Gaskets in unused lids should work well for at least 5 years after manufacture but may fail to seal after longer storage. To ensure a good seal, examine each lid, and don't use any that are old, dented, or deformed or that have gaps or other defects in the sealing gasket. Preheat the lids according to the manufacturer's directions.

After you've filled your jars, proceed as follows: Release air bubbles by inserting a flat plastic (not metal) spatula between the food and the jar. Slowly turn the jar while moving the spatula up and down; this will allow air bubbles to escape. (It is not necessary to release air bubbles when canning jam, jelly, or juice.)

Check the headspace, and add or remove a little food if needed. Then clean the jar rim with a dampened paper towel, because food particles on the rim could cause a seal to fail. Place the preheated lid, gasket down, onto the cleaned rim. Then fit the metal screw band over the flat lid. Tighten the band, but don't force it. When lids are too loose, liquid can escape from the jars during processing, and seals can fail. When lids are too tight, air can't escape during processing, and food may discolor during storage. Overtightening can also cause lids to buckle and jars to break, especially when raw-packed jars are processed in a pressure canner.

You shouldn't retighten the screw bands after processing the jars; this could tear the gaskets. Just let the jars stand until they're cool. As a jar cools, its contents contract. This contraction pulls the lid firmly against the jar, forming a strong vacuum. Once the jars are cool, you can remove the screw bands; they aren't needed during storage. When left on the jars, in fact, screw bands often rust and become difficult to remove. If you wash and dry your screw bands and store them in a dry place, you'll be able to use them many times (with new flat lids).

RECOMMENDED CANNERS

Equipment for heat-processing home-canned food is of 2 main types—boiling-water canners and pressure canners. Most are designed to hold 7 one-quart jars or 8 to 9 pints. Small pressure canners hold only 4 one-quart jars; some large pressure canners hold 18 pint jars in 2 layers but only 7 one-quart jars. Saucepan-size pressure cookers are not recommended for use in canning.

Pressure canners are used to eliminate the botulism risk in low-acid foods. Although pressure canners can be used for processing acid foods, boiling-water canners are recommended for this purpose, because they work faster. Whereas a pressure canner would require 55 to 100 minutes to process a load of jars, the total time for processing most acid foods in boiling water ranges from 25 to 60 minutes. A boiling-water canner loaded with filled jars requires about 20 to 30 minutes of heating before its water begins to boil. A loaded pressure canner requires about 12 to 15 minutes of heating before it begins to vent, 10 minutes of venting, 5 minutes to pressurize, 8 to 10 minutes of processing, and, finally, 20 to 60 minutes to cool before the jars can be removed.

BOILING-WATER CANNERS

Made of aluminum or porcelain-covered steel, these kettles come with fitted lids and removable wire racks with handles. A canner must be deep enough that the jars will be covered by at least 1 inch of boiling water during processing. Some boiling-water canners have flat bottoms; others have ridged bottoms. On a gas range, the bottom can be flat or ridged. If you're using a canner on an electric range, however, the bottom should be flat. To ensure uniform processing of all jars in a boiling-water canner on an electric range, the canner should be no more than 4 inches wider in diameter than the element on which it is heated.

USING A BOILING-WATER CANNER

Follow these steps for successful boiling-water canning:

1. Before you start preparing your food, fill the canner halfway with clean water. This is approximately the level needed for a full load of pint jars.

2. Heat the water to 140°F if you're raw-packing or to 180°F if you're hot-packing. Start preparing the food while the water heats.

3. Load the filled jars, fitted with lids and screw bands, into the canner rack. Use the handles to lower the rack into the water, or put the rack in the bottom of the canner and fill it, one jar at a time, using a jar lifter. When using a jar lifter, make sure you grasp the jar below the neck. Keep the jar upright at all times; tilting it could cause food to spill into the sealing area between the rim and the lid.

4. Add more boiling water, if needed, so the water level in the canner is at least 1 inch above the jar tops. For process times of more than 30 minutes, the water level should be at least 2 inches above the jar tops.

5. Turn the heat to high, cover the canner with its lid, and heat until the water in the canner boils vigorously.

6. Begin timing the processing.

7. Keep the canner covered throughout the processing. You can lower the heat a little, but maintain a boil. **If the water stops boiling at any time during processing, bring the water back to a vigorous boil, and begin the timing over from the beginning.**

8. When the jars have been boiled for the recommended time, turn off the heat and remove the canner lid. Wait 5 minutes before removing the jars.

9. Using a jar lifter, remove the jars and place them on a towel or rack, leaving at least 1 inch of space between the jars. Let the jars cool undisturbed at room temperature for 12 to 24 hours.

PRESSURE CANNERS

Pressure canners for home use have been extensively redesigned in recent years. Models made before the 1970s were heavy-walled kettles with clamp-on or twist-on lids. Each was fitted with a dial gauge, a vent port (steam vent) in the form of a petcock or counterweight, and a safety fuse. Modern pressure canners are lightweight, thin-walled kettles; most have turn-on lids. A modern pressure canner has a jar rack, a gasket, a dial or weighted gauge, an automatic vent-cover lock, a vent port to be closed with a counterweight or weighted gauge, and a safety fuse. To ensure that your old or new canner is safe to use, make sure it has Underwriter's Laboratory (UL) approval.

Pressure does not destroy microorganisms, but high temperatures do—if they are applied for a sufficient time. Successfully destroying all of the microorganisms that are capable of growing in canned food relies on the temperature obtained in pure steam, free of air. At sea level, a canner that is operated at a gauge pressure of 10.5 pounds provides an internal temperature of 240°F, the minimum temperature needed to destroy microorganisms in 20 to 100 minutes.

Two serious errors in pressure canning occur because:

1. Canner gauges measure not absolute pressure but the difference between internal and external pressures. At the same gauge reading, therefore, internal canner temperatures are lower at higher altitudes than at sea level. To correct this error, pressure must be increased for canning at higher altitudes, as specified in this guide.

2. Air trapped in a pressure canner lowers the temperature obtained at 5, 10, or 15 pounds of pressure and results in underprocessing. The highest volume of air trapped in a canner occurs in processing raw-packed foods in dial-gauge canners. These canners do not vent air during processing. To be safe, all types of pressure canners must be vented for 10 minutes before they are pressurized.

To vent a newer model of pressure canner, simply leave the vent port uncovered. On some older models, you must manually open the petcock. Heating the filled canner with its lid locked in place boils the water in the canner and generates steam that escapes through the petcock or vent port, drawing out residual air. When steam begins escaping, set a timer for 10 minutes. After the venting has continued for 10 minutes, pressurize the canner by closing the petcock or placing the counterweight or weighted gauge over the vent port.

Weighted-gauge pressure canners exhaust tiny amounts of air and steam each time the gauge rocks or jiggles during processing. These gauges control pressure precisely and need neither watching during processing nor checking for accuracy. The sound of the weight rocking or jiggling indicates that the canner is maintaining the recommended pressure. The single disadvantage of weighted-gauge canners is that they cannot correct precisely for higher altitudes. At altitudes above 1,000 feet, they must be operated at canner pressures of 10 instead of 5, or 15 instead of 10, PSI.

Dial gauges should be checked for accuracy before use each year. Readings that are higher than they should be can cause underprocessing and make canned food unsafe. Low readings can cause overprocessing. If the gauge reads up to 2 pounds high or low, adjust the pressure accordingly. If the gauge is off by more than 2 pounds—particularly if the gauge reads high—you should replace it. Every pound of pressure is important in attaining a safe processing temperature. Many county Cooperative Extension offices (see the box on page 47) provide a gauge-checking service. If the service isn't available in your area, contact the pressure-canner manufacturer for other options.

If the gasket of a pressure canner gets nicked or dried out, steam may leak during pressurization. Handle your gasket carefully, and clean it after use according to the manufacturer's directions. Gaskets on older-model canners may require a light coat of vegetable oil once per year. Gaskets on newer-model canners are prelubricated at the factory and do not benefit from oiling. Check the instructions that came with your canner if you're not sure whether your gasket has been prelubricated.

The safety fuse on a pressure-canner lid is a thin metal insert or rubber plug designed to relieve excessive pressure from the canner. Try to avoid scratching the fuse while you're cleaning the lid.

Replacement gauges and other canner parts are available at some stores that sell canning equipment as well as from canner manufacturers. When ordering parts, give your canner's model number and describe the parts needed.

USING A PRESSURE CANNER

Follow these steps for successful pressure canning:

1. Pour 2 to 3 inches of hot water (or more if the recipe calls for it) into the canner. Using a jar lifter positioned securely below the neck of the jar, place each filled jar on the canner rack inside the canner. Keep the jars upright at all times. When the canner is loaded, fasten the lid securely.

2. Leave the weight off the vent port, or open the petcock. Turn the burner beneath the canner to its highest setting.

3. When steam begins to flow freely from the open petcock or vent port, maintain the high heat setting. Let the steam flow continuously for 10 minutes, then place the weight on the vent port or close the petcock. The canner will pressurize during the next 3 to 5 minutes.

4. When the pressure reading on the dial gauge indicates that the recommended pressure has been reached, or when the weighted gauge begins to jiggle or rock as the canner manufacturer describes, start timing the processing.

5. Regulate the heat under the canner to maintain a steady pressure at or slightly above the specified gauge level. Quick or large pressure variations during processing could cause the jars to lose liquid. If your canner has a weighted gauge, follow the manufacturer's directions to maintain the desired pressure. **If at any time the pressure falls below the recommended level, bring the canner back to the recommended pressure, and begin timing the processing over from the beginning.**

6. When the processing time is up, turn off the heat. Remove the canner from the heat, if possible, and let it depressurize. Don't cool the canner by running cold water over it or opening the vent port before the canner is fully depressurized. This could cause the jars to lose liquid and the seals to fail. Forced cooling could also warp the

lid of an older-model canner, and the warping could cause steam leaks. If your canner has no dial gauge, time the depressurization. Standard-size, heavy-walled canners require about 30 minutes to depressurize when loaded with pint jars and 45 minutes when loaded with quarts. Newer, thin-walled canners cool more rapidly and are equipped with vent locks. You can tell that one of these canners is depressurized when its vent-lock piston drops to a normal position.

7. After the canner is depressurized, remove the weight from the vent port or open the petcock. Wait 10 minutes, unfasten the lid, and remove it carefully. Lift the lid with the top toward you so that the steam does not burn your face.

8. Remove the jars with a jar lifter, and place them on a towel or rack, leaving at least 1 inch of space between them. Let the jars sit undisturbed at room temperature for 12 to 24 hours.

SELECTING THE CORRECT PROCESSING TIME

When you're using a boiling-water canner, the correct processing time depends on the kind of produce you're canning, how you're packing it, what size jars you're using, and your altitude. When you're using a pressure canner, the correct processing time depends on these same factors as well as on the pressure at which you're processing the jars.

To destroy microorganisms in acid foods processed in a boiling-water canner, you must:

- *Process the jars for the correct number of minutes in boiling water.*

- *Add time if your altitude is above 1,000 feet.*

- *Let the jars cool at room temperature, never in cold water.*

To destroy microorganisms in low-acid foods processed in a pressure canner, you must:

- *Exhaust the canner properly: Let steam flow continuously for 10 minutes before placing a weight on the vent port or closing the petcock.*

- *Process the jars using the correct time and pressure specified for your altitude.*

- *Allow the canner to cool at room temperature—never in cold water—until the canner is completely depressurized.*

PROCESSING-TIME AND PRESSURE TABLES

This guide includes tables that indicate processing times (and canner pressures, when applicable) with altitude adjustments for each type of canned food. Processing times for half-pint and pint jars are the same, as are times for 1½-pint and quart jars.

For some products to be pressure-canned, you have a choice of processing at 5, 10, or 15 PSI. In these cases, choose the canner pressure you wish to use and match it with your pack style (raw or hot) and jar size to find the correct processing time.

The following examples show how to select the proper processing time or pressure for each type of canner—boiling-water canner, dial-gauge pressure canner, and weighted-gauge pressure canner.

EXAMPLE A: BOILING-WATER CANNER

Suppose you are going to process hot-packed peaches in quart jars at 2,500 feet above sea level using a boiling-water canner. First, select the processing table for boiling-water canners. Then, in the Table for Example A, find the processing time for (1) the style of pack (hot), (2) the jar size (quart), and (3) the altitude where you live (1,001 to 3,000 feet). The appropriate processing time is 30 minutes.

Table for Example A Recommended process time for peaches in a boiling-water canner					
		Process time at altitudes of			
Style of pack	**Jar size**	**0– 1,000 ft**	**1,001– 3,000 ft**	**3,001– 6,000 ft**	**Above 6,000 ft**
Hot	Pints	20 mins	25 mins	30 mins	35 mins
	Quarts	25 mins	30 mins	35 mins	40 mins
Raw	Pints	25 mins	30 mins	35 mins	40 mins
	Quarts	30 mins	35 mins	40 mins	45 mins

EXAMPLE B: DIAL-GAUGE PRESSURE CANNER

Suppose you are going to process hot-packed peaches in quart jars at 2,500 feet above sea level using a dial-gauge pressure canner. First, select the processing table for dial-gauge pressure canners. Then, in the Table for Example B, you'll see that the processing time, 10 minutes, is the same for both hot- and raw-packed peaches and for both pint and quart jars. The correct pressure, however, varies depending on your altitude. Because you live at an altitude between 2,001 and 4,000 feet, you should select a pressure of 7 pounds for the 10-minute processing.

Table for Example B
Recommended process time for peaches in a dial-gauge pressure canner

Style of pack	Jar size	Process time	Canner pressure (PSI) at altitudes of			
			0–2,000 ft	2,001–4,000 ft	4,001–6,000 ft	6,001–8,000 ft
Hot or Raw	Pints or Quarts	10 min	6 lb	7 lb	8 lb	9 lb

EXAMPLE C: WEIGHTED-GAUGE PRESSURE CANNER

Suppose you are going to process hot-packed peaches in quart jars at 2,500 feet above sea level using a weighted-gauge pressure canner. First, select the processing table for weighted-gauge pressure canners. In the Table for Example C, the processing time, 10 minutes, is the same for both hot- and raw-packed peaches and for both pint and quart jars. But the correct pressure, again, varies depending on your altitude. Because you live at an altitude above 1,000 feet, you should select a pressure of 10 pounds for the 10-minute processing.

Table for Example C
Recommended process time for peaches in a weighted-gauge pressure canner

Style of pack	Jar size	Process time	Canner pressure (PSI) at altitudes of	
			0–1,000 ft	Above 1,000 ft
Hot or Raw	Pints or Quarts	10 min	5 lb	10 lb

COOLING JARS

When you remove hot jars from a canner, place them on a rack or towel with at least 1 inch of space between them. Do not retighten the screw bands; this could tear the gaskets and cause the seals to fail. Let the jars cool at room temperature for 12 to 24 hours. In raw-packed jars, the headspace will be noticeably larger after the cooling period. That's because during the processing of raw-packed foods, air is exhausted and the food shrinks.

In raw-packed jars, the headspace will be noticeably larger after the cooling period. That's because during the processing of raw-packed foods, air is exhausted and the food shrinks.

Sometimes a jar loses liquid during processing. In this case, don't open the jar to add more liquid. The leakage may keep the jar from sealing, or it may not. If the jar seals, it can be safely stored.

TESTING JAR SEALS

After letting the jars cool for 12 to 24 hours, remove the screw bands. Then test the seals in any of the following ways:

1. Press the middle of the lid with your finger or thumb. If the lid springs up when you release your finger, the lid is unsealed.
2. Tap the lid with the bottom of a teaspoon. If the jar is sealed, you'll hear a ringing, high-pitched sound. If you hear a dull sound, either the lid is unsealed or food is stuck on the underside of the lid. (If you suspect the latter, test the seal again with either of the other testing methods.)
3. Hold the jar at eye level, and look across the lid. The lid should be slightly concave (curved inward) in the center. If the center of the lid is flat or bulging upward, the lid may not be sealed.

REPROCESSING UNSEALED JARS

If a lid has failed to seal, you can process the jar again provided that no more than 24 hours have passed since the first processing. Remove the lid, and check the rim of the jar for nicks. Change the jar if there are any nicks; otherwise, just clean the rim with a dampened paper towel. Add a new lid, prepared according to the manufacturer's instructions, and process the jar as before.

If only 1 or 2 jars have failed to seal, you might not want to bother with reprocessing. If that's the case, you can adjust the headspace to 1½ inches (to allow the food to expand), and store the capped jar in the freezer. Or, if you'll consume the food within several days, you can simply cap the jar and place it in the refrigerator.

STORING CANNED FOODS

If the lids are tightly sealed on your cooled jars, wash the outside of the lids and jars to remove any food residue, and then rinse and dry the jars. (Remember that there's no need to put the screw bands back on for storage.) Label the jars with the contents and the date you processed them, and store them in a clean, cool, dark, dry place. Don't put them in direct sunlight; near hot pipes or ducts, a range, or a furnace; or anywhere else where the temperature could rise above 95°F. And don't store them under a sink or in any other space where dampness could corrode the lids and break the seals. In any of these conditions, the food would lose quality in a few weeks or months and might even spoil.

If possible, you should also avoid storing your filled jars in an uninsulated attic or other location where they are liable to freeze. Accidental freezing of canned foods will not cause spoilage unless the jars become unsealed. However, freezing and thawing could soften the foods. If you must store your jars where they might freeze, wrap them in newspapers, place them in heavy cartons, and cover the cartons with more newspapers or with blankets.

IDENTIFYING AND HANDLING SPOILED CANNED FOOD

Do not taste food from a jar with an unsealed lid or canned food that shows signs of spoilage. When you take a jar of your home-canned food out of storage, make sure the lid is still firmly attached and has a concave center (see option 3 under "Testing jar seals" on page 67). Spoilage bacteria and yeast produce gas, which makes the lid swell and breaks the jar seal. Such swelling is particularly noticeable if the screw band is still attached.

Check for other signs of spoilage by holding the jar upright at eye level and rotating it. Look for streaks of dried food on the outside surface, originating at the top of the jar. Look also for rising air bubbles within the jar and any strange coloring of the contents.

When you open the jar, sniff for odd odors. Look for spurting liquid and cottonlike mold growth (white, blue, black, or green) on the top surface of the food and the underside of the lid.

Spoiled low-acid foods and tomatoes may exhibit different signs and, often, few signs at all, even though they may harbor the toxin that causes botulism. That is why it is so vital to follow the proper canning procedures for low-acid foods as spelled out in this guide. And you should suspect a low-acid or tomato food is spoiled if:

- *The food was not properly processed in a pressure canner, following the steps outlined in this guide.*

- *The scientifically researched process time and pressure indicated in this guide for the altitude, type of food, style of pack, and jar size were not used.*

- *The pressure canner's gauge malfunctioned or was inaccurate.*

- *Additional ingredients were used that do not appear in the recipe in this guide, or the proportions of ingredients were altered.*

If you suspect that any jar of low-acid food or tomatoes is spoiled, treat it as if it contains botulinum toxin. Botulinum toxin can be fatal, whether it is ingested or enters the body through the skin. If the suspect jar is still sealed, put it in a heavy garbage bag, close the bag, and put it in a trash container for disposal in a landfill. If the jar is unsealed, fully open, or leaking, detoxify the food before disposing of it, as follows:

1. While wearing disposable rubber or heavy plastic gloves, carefully place the suspect containers—with the food still inside—on their sides in a boiling-water canner or stockpot that has a capacity of at least 8 quarts. Be sure to put the lid and, if it was left on during storage, the screw band into the pot as well.

2. Thoroughly wash your gloved hands.

3. Taking care to avoid splashing, add enough water to the pot to cover the containers by at least 1 inch. Place a lid on the pot, and heat the water to boiling. Boil for 30 minutes to ensure that the food, jars, and lids are fully detoxified.

4. When the pot has cooled, put the jars, lids, bands, and food in the trash for disposal in a landfill.

5. Clean up the area. Wearing rubber or heavy plastic gloves, treat all work surfaces, equipment, and clothing that may have come in contact with the suspect foods with a fresh solution of 1 part unscented liquid household chlorine bleach (5 percent to 6 percent sodium hypochlorite) to 5 parts clean water. (Bleach is an irritant, so ventilate the room, and don't let the solution come in contact with your skin or eyes.) Spray or wet the contaminated surfaces with the bleach solution, and wait 30 minutes. Then wipe up the treated spills with paper towels, and put the paper towels in a plastic bag before putting them in the trash. Next, apply the bleach solution to all surfaces and equipment again.Wait another 30 minutes, and then rinse with clean water. As a last step, thoroughly wash all counters, containers, equipment, and clothing. When the cleaning process is complete, discard your gloves in the trash.

CANNED FOODS FOR SPECIAL DIETS

Because canned foods for special diets are expensive to buy, many people want to prepare their own. Some low-sugar and low-salt foods can be easily and safely canned at home. The color, flavor, and texture of these home-canned foods, however, may be a little different from what you expect.

CANNING WITHOUT SUGAR

When canning regular fruits without sugar, it is very important to select fully ripe but still firm fruits of the best quality. Hot-pack the fruits but use water or unsweetened fruit juice instead of sugar syrup. It's best to use juice from the same fruit that you're canning, but a combination of unsweetened apple, pineapple, and white grape juices is also good for this purpose. Follow the procedures for fruits canned in sugar syrup as you adjust the headspace of the jars, attach the lids and screw bands, and process the jars.

Splenda® is a sugar substitute currently available that can be added to juice or water when canning fruits. Other sugar substitutes, if desired, should be added at serving time.

CANNING WITHOUT SALT

To can tomatoes or low-acid vegetables for a low-sodium diet, follow the procedures given in their respective chapters, but omit the salt. In these recipes, salt is included for seasoning, not to ensure safety.

If you'd like to use a salt substitute with your canned tomatoes or low-acid vegetables, add it just before serving.

CANNING FRUIT-BASED BABY FOODS

You can prepare any chunk-style or puréed fruit with or without sugar, using the procedures for fruit in the next chapter. Half-pint jars are generally preferable for baby food, but you can use pint jars if you prefer. Use the processing times in the table that follows.

Recommended process time for fruit-based baby foods in a boiling-water canner				
		Process time at altitudes of		
Style of pack	Jar size	0–1,000 ft	1,001–6,000 ft	Above 6,000 ft
Hot	Pints	20 min	25 min	30 min

Proper processing times have not been determined for home-canning pureed vegetables. **If you want to can vegetables for your baby, do so using the standard procedures that are described in Chapter 7, and then purée the vegetables at serving time. Heat the puréed food to boiling; simmer for 10 minutes; and let the food cool briefly before feeding it to your baby. Store any unused portion in the refrigerator. For best quality, use the remainder within 2 days.**

FERMENTED & FRESH PICKLED VEGETABLES

Pickling is a method of preserving food that uses acid to prevent the growth of undesirable bacteria, including illness-inducing ones. This chapter discusses two basic pickling methods, one using fermentation and the other vinegar.

PREPARING PICKLED FOODS

The many varieties of fermented and fresh pickled vegetables are classified by ingredients and method of preparation:

- **Fermented pickles** *and* **sauerkraut** *are cured about 3 weeks, during which colors and flavors change. Brine (salt water) facilitates fermentation—which creates the necessary acidic environment—while discouraging growth of harmful bacteria.*

- **Fresh-pack** *or* **quick-process pickles** *are not fermented, although sometimes the vegetables are brined several hours or overnight before being covered with vinegar and seasonings. Vinegar creates the acidic environment.*

- **Relishes** *are made from chopped fruits and vegetables cooked with seasonings and vinegar.*

The acidity level in a pickled food is important to its safety, taste, and texture. There must be a minimum, uniform level of acid throughout the jar contents to prevent the growth of *Clostridium botulinum* bacteria.

To ensure your pickled foods are safe:

- *Don't alter the proportions of vinegar, food, and water in a recipe.*

- *Don't use vinegar of unknown acidity.*

- *Use only recipes with ingredients in tested proportions.*

SELECTION OF FRESH CUCUMBERS

The favorite vegetable to be pickled is, of course, the cucumber.

QUANTITY: A quart jar holds about 2 pounds of cucumbers. You'll therefore need about 14 pounds to fill 7 quart jars and about 9 pounds to fill 9 pint jars. A bushel of pickling cucumbers weighs 48 pounds and yields 16 to 24 quarts of cucumber pickles.

QUALITY: Select firm pickling cucumbers no longer than about 4 inches. Choose cucumbers about 1½ inches long for gherkins and about 4 inches long for dills. Use oddly shaped and oversize cucumbers for relish or bread-and-butter pickles.

TIP

When making fermented or fresh-pack cucumber pickles or chopping cucumbers for relish, remove and discard a 1/16-inch slice from the blossom end. Cucumber blossoms contain an enzyme that can cause pickles to soften.

OTHER INGREDIENTS

Choose salt labeled for use in canning or pickling. Other salts like table salt contain anticaking additives that can make pickle brine cloudy. Flake salt varies in density, so it shouldn't be used with recipes (like those in this guide) designed and tested using volume measurements for granulated salt. The most common sweeteners added to pickles are granulated white sugar and brown sugar. Corn syrup and honey, except when called for in reliable recipes, could produce undesirable flavors. For pickles made with vinegar, distilled white and cider vinegars of 5 percent acidity (50 grain) are recommended. Distilled vinegar is preferred when a light color is desirable.

CONTAINERS AND WEIGHTS FOR FERMENTING PICKLES

Ferment vegetables in a crock, glass jar, or food-grade plastic container. A gallon jar holds about 5 pounds of fresh cabbage or cucumbers; a 5-gallon crock is ideal for fermenting about 25 pounds. You can make sauerkraut in a half-gallon or even quart Mason jar, if you like, but by doing so you'll risk more loss from spoilage. A 1- to 3-gallon non-food-grade plastic container will do for brining vegetables if you line it with a clean, food-grade plastic bag. **Do not use a garbage bag or trash liner for this purpose.** While fermenting, cabbage and cucumbers must be kept 1 to 2 inches under the surface of the brine. You can hold them down with a dinner plate or glass pie plate that is slightly smaller than the container opening.

> **TIP**
>
> When preparing fresh produce for pickling, measure or weigh amounts carefully. The proportion of fresh food to other ingredients will affect flavor and, in many instances, safety.

Weight the plate with 2 to 3 capped quart jars filled with water, and cover the container opening with a clean, heavy towel to help prevent contamination from insects and molds. Or, instead of using a plate and jars of water, you can weight the vegetables with a clean food-grade plastic bag filled with 1½ tablespoons canning and pickling salt for each quart of water. Seal the bag, and make sure it fills the top of the container. Freezer bags sold for packaging turkeys are suitable for use with 5-gallon containers. Before you start, wash the fermentation container, the plate, and the jars to be used as weights in hot sudsy water, and rinse them well.

FIRMING AGENTS

Alum may be safely used to firm fermented pickles, but it isn't necessary and isn't called for in this guide. Alum doesn't improve the firmness of quick-process pickles. The calcium in lime, on the other hand, definitely firms pickles. Fresh cucumbers can be soaked in a mixture of food-grade lime and water for 12 to 24 hours before they are pickled. But with lime's high pH, excess amounts must be removed to make the pickles safe. To remove excess lime, drain off the lime water, rinse the cucumbers, then soak them in fresh water for 1 hour. Repeat the rinsing and soaking twice more. Another way to keep cucumber pickles firm—and to prevent spoilage—is to use low-temperature pasteurization (see next page).

SPOILAGE PREVENTION

Pickled foods are subject to spoilage from microorganisms, particularly yeasts and molds, and to enzymes that can affect flavor, color, and texture. Selecting fresh, firm vegetables free of spoilage; using standard canning jars and self-sealing lids; and processing jars of pickled vegetables in a boiling-water canner will prevent both. The specified processing times and procedures vary according to the acidity of the pickled food and the size of the food pieces.

LOW-TEMPERATURE PASTEURIZATION

Some pickles are best pasteurized not through boiling-water processing or pressure canning but at a lower temperature, as follows: Put the jars into a canner filled halfway with warm water (120° to 140°F). Add enough hot water to cover the jars by 1 inch. Heat the water to 180°F, and hold it between 180° and 185°F for 30 minutes. Use an accurate thermometer to ensure the water temperature remains in that range the entire time. **Use low-temperature pasteurization only when a recipe calls for it.**

PICKLES WITH REDUCED SALT CONTENT

You can safely reduce or eliminate the salt in recipes for fresh-pack pickles, although the texture and flavor may be slightly, but noticeably, altered. You may want to make only a small quantity of reduced-salt pickles at first to see if you like them.

In fermented pickles and sauerkraut, however, the salt is vital to safety. Salt encourages growth of the desirable bacteria responsible for fermentation while inhibiting growth of dangerous ones. **Do not reduce the amount of salt or use reduced-sodium salt in recipes for sauerkraut or fermented pickles.**

FERMENTED PICKLED VEGETABLES

DILL PICKLES

Use the following quantities for each gallon that your pickling container will hold.

4 lbs 4-inch-long pickling cucumbers
2 tbsp dill seed or 4 to 5 heads fresh or dry dill
2 cloves garlic (optional)
2 dried red peppers (optional)
2 tsp whole mixed pickling spices (optional)
¼ cup vinegar (5% acidity)
8 cups water
½ cup canning and pickling salt

PROCEDURE: Wash the cucumbers, and cut ¹⁄₁₆ inch off the blossom ends. If the cucumbers have stems, trim them to ¼ inch. Put half the dill, garlic, peppers, and spices on the bottom of your pickling container. Add the cucumbers and the remaining dill, garlic, peppers, and spices. Combine the vinegar and water in a bowl or pot, and dissolve the salt in the liquid. Pour this brine over the cucumbers. Cover and weight the cucumbers (see pages 79–80), and lay a towel over the container.

Combine the vinegar and water in a bowl or pot, and dissolve the salt in the liquid. Pour this brine over the cucumbers. Cover and weight the cucumbers (see pages 79–80), and lay a towel over the container. Store it where the temperature will remain at about 70° to 75°F for the duration of the fermentation, about 3 to 4 weeks. Temperatures as low as 55°F are acceptable, but at lower temperatures, fermentation will take 5 to 6 weeks. Avoid temperatures above 80°F, which can make pickles soft. If you have weighted the cucumbers with a brine-filled bag, do not disturb the container until fermentation is complete (when the bubbling ceases). If you've used jars as weights, check the container several times a week, and promptly remove any scum or mold on the surface. **If the pickles become soft or slimy or develop a disagreeable odor, throw them out.**

When the pickles are fully fermented, you can store them in the pickling container in the refrigerator for about 4 to 6 months, provided you promptly remove any surface scum or mold that develops. Or you may can your pickles. To do so, pour the brine into a pot, heat it slowly to a boil, and simmer it for 5 minutes. Filter the brine through a paper coffee filter, if you prefer. Then fill hot quart or pint jars with the cold pickles and hot brine, leaving ½ inch headspace. Remove the air bubbles, and adjust the headspace if needed. Wipe the rims of the jars with a clean, dampened paper towel; apply the preheated lids and screw bands; and process the jars according to the table that follows, or use the low-temperature pasteurization treatment.

Dill Pickles Recommended process time in a boiling-water canner				
Style of pack	Jar size	Process time at altitudes of		
		0–1,000 ft	1,001–6,000 ft	Above 6,000 ft
Raw	Pints	10 min	15	20
	Quarts	15	20	25

SAUERKRAUT

25 lbs cabbage
¾ cup canning and pickling salt

QUALITY: For the best sauerkraut, use firm cabbage heads, and start preparing them for kraut between 24 and 48 hours after harvest.

YIELD: About 9 quarts

PROCEDURE: Work with about 5 pounds of cabbage at a time. Remove and discard outer leaves. Rinse the heads under cold running water, and drain. Quarter and core the heads. Shred or slice the cabbage to the thickness of a quarter. Put the shredded cabbage in the fermentation container, and add 3 tablespoons of the salt. With your hands, mix the cabbage and salt thoroughly. Pack the cabbage firmly in the container. Repeat the shredding, salting, and packing until all the cabbage is packed, but don't fill the container to the top; the cabbage should be at least 4 inches below the rim. The salt will begin drawing liquid from the cabbage at once, forming a brine. If the brine doesn't cover the cabbage when you're finished packing it, combine 1½ tablespoons of salt with a quart of boiling water, and let the solution cool. Add enough of this brine to cover the cabbage. Then weight the cabbage (see pages 79–80), and cover the container. Store the container where the temperature will remain at about 70° to 75°F for the duration of fermentation, about 3 to 4 weeks. Temperatures as low as 60°F are acceptable, but at lower temperatures, fermentation will take about 5 to 6 weeks. At temperatures below 60°F, the cabbage may not ferment. Temperatures above 75°F can make kraut soft. If you've weighted the cabbage with a brine-filled bag, do not disturb the container until fermentation is complete (when bubbling ceases). If you've used jars as weights, check the kraut 2 to 3 times each week, and remove any scum that forms.

Fully fermented kraut can be kept in the refrigerator, tightly covered, for several months, or it can be canned. To hot-pack the kraut, slowly bring it and the brine to a boil in a large pot, stirring frequently, then remove the pot from the heat. Pack the hot or raw kraut with its brine into hot pint or quart jars, leaving ½ inch headspace. Remove the air bubbles, and adjust the headspace if needed. Wipe the rims of the jars with a clean, dampened paper towel; apply the preheated lids and screw bands; and process the jars as indicated in the table that follows.

Sauerkraut					
Recommended process time in a boiling-water canner					
Style of pack	Jar size	**Process time at altitudes of**			
		0–1,000 ft	1,001–3,000 ft	3,001–6,000 ft	Above 6,000 ft
Hot	Pints	10 min	15	15	20
	Quarts	15	20	20	25
Raw	Pints	20	25	30	35
	Quarts	25	30	35	40

FRESH PICKLED CUCUMBERS (PICKLES)

BREAD-AND-BUTTER PICKLES

In this recipe, you can substitute slender zucchini or yellow summer squash for the cucumbers. The squash should be 1 to 1½ inches in diameter.

6 lbs 4- to 5-inch-long pickling cucumbers

8 cups thinly sliced onions (about 3 pounds)

½ cup canning and pickling salt

4 cups vinegar (5% acidity)

4½ cups sugar

2 tbsp mustard seed

1½ tbsp celery seed

1 tbsp ground turmeric

YIELD: About 8 pints

PROCEDURE: Wash the cucumbers, and cut 1/16 inch off the blossom ends. Cut the cucumbers crosswise into 3/16-inch-thick slices. Combine the cucumbers and onions in a large bowl, sprinkle the salt over them, and cover with 2 inches of crushed or cubed ice. Refrigerate the bowl for 3 to 4 hours, adding more ice as needed. At the end of this period, combine the vinegar, sugar, mustard seed, celery seed, and turmeric in a large pot. Bring the mixture to a boil, and boil it for 10 minutes. Drain the cucumbers and onions, discarding any remaining ice. Add the vegetables to the pot, and slowly heat the contents to a boil. Fill hot pint or quart jars with the hot vegetables and the liquid, leaving 1/2 inch headspace. Remove the air bubbles, and adjust the headspace if needed. Wipe the rims of the jars with a clean, dampened paper towel; apply the preheated lids and screw bands; and process the jars according to the table that follows, or use the low-temperature pasteurization treatment (page 81). Store the cooled jars for at least 4 weeks to develop the best flavor.

Bread-and-Butter Pickles				
Recommended process time in a boiling-water canner				
		Process time at altitudes of		
Style of pack	Jar size	0–1,000 ft	1,001–6,000 ft	Above 6,000 ft
Hot	Pints or Quarts	10 min	15	20

VARIATION: For firmer pickles, mix 1 cup of pickling lime and 1/2 cup of salt with 1 gallon of water in a 2- to 3-gallon crock or enamelware container. **Avoid inhaling the lime dust.** Soak the freshly washed and sliced cucumbers in the lime water for 12 to 24 hours, stirring occasionally. Drain and rinse the cucumbers, and soak them for 1 hour in fresh cold water. Repeat the rinsing and soaking twice more, handling the slices carefully (they will be brittle). Drain them well before proceeding with the recipe.

QUICK FRESH DILL PICKLES

8 lbs 3- to 5-inch-long pickling cucumbers

1¼ cups canning and pickling salt

1½ quarts vinegar (5% acidity)

¼ cup sugar

2 tbsp whole mixed pickling spices

About 3 tbsp mustard seed

About 12 fresh dill heads or 4 tbsp dill seed

YIELD: About 4 quarts

PROCEDURE: Wash the cucumbers, and cut 1⁄16 inch off the blossom ends. If the cucumbers have stems, trim them to ¼ inch. Dissolve ¾ cup of the salt in 2 gallons of water. Pour this brine over the cucumbers, let them stand 12 hours, then drain them. In a pot, combine the vinegar, the remaining ½ cup salt, the sugar, and 2 quarts of water. Tie the mixed pickling spices in a spice bag or 2 layers of cheesecloth. Add the spice bundle to the pot, and heat the contents to a boil. Fill hot quart or pint jars with the raw cucumbers, and add 2 teaspoons of mustard seed and either 3 dill heads or 1 tablespoon of dill seed per quart. Cover the cucumbers with the hot pickling liquid, leaving ½ inch headspace. Remove the air bubbles, and adjust the headspace if needed. Wipe the rims of jars with a clean, dampened paper towel; apply the preheated lids and screw bands; and process the jars according to the table that follows, or use the low-temperature pasteurization treatment.

Quick Fresh Dill Pickles Recommended process time in a boiling-water canner				
		Process time at altitudes of		
Style of pack	Jar size	0–1,000 ft	1,001–6,000 ft	Above 6,000 ft
Raw	Pints	10 min	15	20
	Quarts	15	20	25

SWEET GHERKIN PICKLES

7 lbs cucumbers, each no longer than 1½ inches

½ cup canning and pickling salt

6 cups vinegar (5% acidity)

8 cups sugar

¾ tsp ground turmeric

2 tsp celery seeds

2 tsp whole mixed pickling spices

2 one-inch-long cinnamon sticks

½ tsp fennel seeds (optional)

2 tsp vanilla extract (optional)

YIELD: About 6 to 7 pints

PROCEDURE: Day 1. Wash the cucumbers, and cut ¹⁄₁₆ inch off the blossom ends. If the cucumbers have stems, trim them to ¼ inch. Put the cucumbers in a large container; cover them with boiling water, and, 6 to 8 hours later, drain off the water. Dissolve ¼ cup of the salt in 6 quarts of fresh boiling water, and pour this brine over the cucumbers.

Day 2. Drain the cucumbers again. Dissolve the remaining ¼ cup of the salt in 6 quarts of fresh boiling water, and pour this brine over the cucumbers.

Day 3. Drain the cucumbers, and prick each with a table fork. In a pot, combine 3 cups of the vinegar, 3 cups of the sugar, the turmeric, the celery seeds, the mixed pickling spices, the cinnamon sticks, and, if you like, the fennel seeds. Bring this mixture to a boil; pour it over the cucumbers; and, 6 to 8 hours later, drain off the pickling syrup into a pot. Add 2 more cups each of the sugar and vinegar, heat the syrup to a boil, and pour it over the pickles.

Day 4. Drain the syrup into a pot. Add 2 more cups of the sugar and 1 more cup of the vinegar, heat the syrup to a boil, and pour it over the pickles. Six to eight hours later, drain the syrup into a pot; add the remaining 1 cup of sugar and the vanilla extract, if you like; and heat the syrup to a boil. Pack the pickles into hot sterilized pint jars (see page 53), and cover them with the hot syrup, leaving ½ inch headspace. Remove the air bubbles, and adjust the headspace if needed. Wipe the rims of the jars with a clean, dampened paper towel; apply the preheated lids and screw bands; and process the jars according to the table that follows, or use the low-temperature pasteurization treatment.

Sweet Gherkin Pickles Recommended process time in a boiling-water canner				
		Process time at altitudes of		
Style of pack	**Jar size**	**0–1,000 ft**	**1,001–6,000 ft**	**Above 6,000 ft**
Raw	Pints	5 min	10	15

OTHER FRESH PICKLED VEGETABLES

PICKLED BEETS

Use beets of uniform size. Before cooking, trim their tops and roots, leaving 1 inch of each to prevent excessive bleeding of color.

7 lbs beets, each 2 to 2½ inches in diameter, trimmed

4 to 6 onions, each 2 to 2½ inches in diameter

4 cups vinegar (5% acidity)

1½ tsp canning and pickling salt

2 cups sugar

2 cups water

2 cinnamon sticks

12 whole cloves

YIELD: About 8 pints

PROCEDURE: Wash the beets thoroughly. Put them into a pot, cover them with boiling water, and cook them until they are tender, about 25 to 30 minutes. Drain and discard the liquid, and let the beets cool in the air. Trim off the remaining roots and stems, and slip off the skins. Slice the beets into ¼-inch-thick rounds, and slice the onions thin. In a pot, combine the vinegar, salt, sugar, and water. Tie the spices in a spice bag or 2 layers of cheesecloth, and add this bundle to the vinegar mixture. Bring the mixture to a boil, then add the sliced beets and onions. Simmer the mixture for 5 minutes. Remove the spice bag. Fill hot pint or quart jars with the beets and onions, and add the hot liquid to the jars, leaving ½ inch headspace. Remove the air bubbles, and adjust the headspace if needed. Wipe the rims of the jars with a clean, dampened paper towel; apply the preheated lids and screw bands; and process the jars as indicated in the table that follows.

Pickled Beets					
Recommended process time in a boiling-water canner					
		Process time at altitudes of			
Style of pack	Jar size	0–1,000 ft	1,001–3,000 ft	3,001–6,000 ft	Above 6,000 ft
Hot	Pints or Quarts	30 min	35	40	45

VARIATION: If the beets are no more than 1½ inches in diameter, you can pickle them whole. Omit the onions, if you prefer.

PICKLED HOT PEPPERS

You can use green or ripe hot peppers, such as Hungarian wax or New Mexican, and green or ripe sweet peppers, such as banana. A mix of colors makes the prettiest pickle. **When handling hot peppers, wear plastic or rubber gloves and avoid touching your eyes or face.**

4 lbs long hot peppers
3 lbs sweet peppers
5 cups vinegar (5% acidity)
1 cup water
4 tsp canning and pickling salt
2 tbsp sugar
2 cloves garlic

YIELD: About 9 pints

PROCEDURE: Wash the peppers. If they're small, leave them whole; if they're large, quarter them. If you leave them whole, cut 2 to 4 slits in each. Blanch the peppers in boiling water or, if the skins are tough, blister them. Do this in a hot oven (400°F) or under a broiler for 6 to 8 minutes or over a gas or electric burner covered with heavy wire mesh for several minutes. Place the blistered peppers in a pan, and cover them with a damp cloth for several minutes before peeling them. If the peppers are whole, flatten them. Pack the peppers into hot pint or half-pint jars, leaving ½ inch headspace. In a saucepan, combine the vinegar, water, salt, sugar, and garlic. Heat the mixture to a boil, reduce the heat, and simmer the mixture for 10 minutes. Remove the garlic. Cover the peppers with the hot liquid, keeping the ½ inch headspace. Remove the air bubbles, and adjust the headspace if needed. Wipe the rims of the jars with a clean, dampened paper towel; apply the preheated lids and screw bands; and process the jars as indicated in the table that follows.

Pickled Hot Peppers				
Recommended process time in a boiling-water canner				
		Process time at altitudes of		
Style of pack	Jar size	0–1,000 ft	1,001–6,000 ft	Above 6,000 ft
Raw	Half-pints or Pints	10 min	15	20

PICKLED VEGETABLE RELISHES

PICCALILLI

6 cups chopped green tomatoes

1½ cups chopped sweet red peppers

1½ cups chopped green peppers

2¼ cups chopped onions

7½ cups chopped cabbage

½ cup canning and pickling salt

4½ cups vinegar (5% acidity)

3 cups brown sugar

3 tbsp whole mixed pickling spices

YIELD: About 9 half-pints

PROCEDURE: In a bowl, combine the chopped vegetables and salt. Cover the vegetables with hot water, and let stand 12 hours. Press in a clean white cloth to remove all excess liquid. In a pot, combine the vinegar and brown sugar. Tie the spices in a spice bag. Add this bundle to the pot, and heat the mixture to a boil. Add vegetables, and boil gently for 30 minutes or until volume is reduced by half. Remove the spice bag. Pack the mixture into hot, sterilized half-pint or pint jars (see page 53), leaving ½ inch headspace. Remove the air bubbles, and adjust the headspace if needed. Wipe the rims of the jars with a clean, dampened paper towel; apply the preheated lids and screw bands; and process the jars as indicated in the following table.

Piccalilli Recommended process time in a boiling-water canner				
		Process time at altitudes of		
Style of pack	Jar size	0–1,000 ft	1,001–6,000 ft	Above 6,000 ft
Hot	Half-pints or Pints	5 min	10	15

PICKLE RELISH

3 quarts chopped cucumbers

3 cups chopped sweet green peppers

3 cups chopped sweet red peppers

1 cup chopped onions

¾ cup canning and pickling salt

4 tsp mustard seed

4 tsp ground turmeric

4 tsp whole allspice

4 tsp whole cloves

2 cups sugar

6 cups distilled white vinegar (5% acidity)

YIELD: About 9 pints

PROCEDURE: Day 1. In a large pot, combine the chopped cucumbers, peppers, and onions with the salt. Top the vegetables with 1 quart of cubed or crushed ice, and pour 2 quarts of water over them. Let the vegetables stand at room temperature for 4 hours. Drain the water, cover the vegetables with fresh ice and water, and let stand for another hour. Drain the water again. Tie the mustard seed, turmeric, allspice, and cloves in a spice bag or 2 layers of cheesecloth. Combine this bundle with the sugar and vinegar in a smaller pot. Heat the mixture to a boil, and pour it over the vegetables. Cover the vegetables, and refrigerate them for 24 hours.

Day 2. Heat the vegetables and their liquid to boiling, and remove the spice bag. Pack the hot vegetables and liquid into hot half-pint or pint jars, leaving ½ inch headspace. Remove the air bubbles, and adjust the headspace if needed. Wipe the rims of the jars with a clean, dampened paper towel; apply the preheated lids and screw bands; and process the jars as indicated in the table that follows.

Pickle Relish				
Recommended process time in a boiling-water canner				
		Process time at altitudes of		
Style of pack	Jar size	0–1,000 ft	1,001–6,000 ft	Above 6,000 ft
Hot	Half-pints or Pints	10 min	15	20

FRUIT & FRUIT PRODUCTS

Adding syrup to canned fruit doesn't prevent spoilage, but it does help in retaining the flavor, color, and shape of the fruit. The tables "Formulas and Uses for Sugar Syrups" (below and on page 98) show quantities of water and sugar needed for syrups of various strengths. For each type of syrup, the tables also give typical uses. Each formula in the table below will make enough syrup for 9 pints or 4 quarts of fruit; the formulas in the table at the top of page 98 will make enough syrup for 7 quarts of fruit.

Many fruits typically packed in heavy syrup are excellent packed in lighter syrups instead, so try lighter syrups if you want fewer calories in the form of added sugar. The "very light" syrup in the tables approximates the natural sugar content of many fruits.

| Formulas and Uses for Sugar Syrups | | | | |
| For a 9-Pint or 4-Quart Load | | | | |
Syrup type	Approx. % sugar	Water (cups)	Sugar (cups)	Fruits commonly packed in this type of syrup
Very light	10	6½	¾	Various. This syrup approximates the natural sugar level in most fruits and adds the fewest calories.
Light	20	5¾	1½	Very sweet fruits. Try a small amount the first time to see if your family likes it.
Medium	30	5¼	2¼	Sweet apples, berries, sweet cherries, grapes.
Heavy	40	5	3¼	Tart apples, apricots, sour cherries, gooseberries, nectarines, peaches, pears, plums.
Very heavy	50	4¼	4¼	Very sour fruits. Try a small amount the first time to see if your family likes it.

Formulas and Uses for Sugar Syrups				
For a 7-Quart Load				
Syrup type	Approx. % sugar	Water (cups)	Sugar (cups)	Fruits commonly packed in this type of syrup
Very light	10	10½	1¼	Various. This syrup approximates the natural sugar level in most fruits and adds the fewest calories.
Light	20	9	2¼	Very sweet fruits. Try a small amount the first time to see if your family likes it.
Medium	30	8¼	3¾	Sweet apples, berries, sweet cherries, grapes.
Heavy	40	7¾	5¼	Tart apples, apricots, sour cherries, gooseberries, nectarines, peaches, pears, plums.
Very heavy	50	6½	6¾	Very sour fruits. Try a small amount the first time to see if your family likes it.

PROCEDURE: Heat the water and sugar together. Bring the syrup to a boil. If you're raw-packing, pour the syrup over the raw fruit in jars. If you're hot-packing, add the fruit to the syrup, reheat the syrup to a boil, and immediately fill the jars with the fruit and syrup.

OTHER SWEETENERS: You can use light corn syrup or mild-flavored honey to replace up to half the sugar called for in the preceding tables. See "Canned foods for special diets," page 73, for further discussion of alternative sweeteners.

APPLE BUTTER

Jonathan, Winesap, Stayman, Golden Delicious, and MacIntosh are among the varieties that make tasty apple butter.

8 lbs apples
2 cups cider
2 cups vinegar
2¼ cups white sugar
2¼ cups packed brown sugar
2 tbsp ground cinnamon
1 tbsp ground cloves

YIELD: About 8 to 9 pints

PROCEDURE: Wash, stem, quarter, and core the apples. Cook them slowly in the cider and vinegar until they are soft. Press the fruit through a colander, food mill, or strainer. Cook the fruit pulp with the white and brown sugar and the spices, stirring frequently. To test for doneness, remove a spoonful and hold it away from the steam for 2 minutes; it is ready if the apple butter remains mounded on the spoon. Or spoon a small quantity onto a plate; if liquid doesn't separate around the edge, the cooking is done. Pour the hot apple butter into sterilized (see page 53) half-pint or pint jars or clean, hot quart jars, leaving ¼ inch headspace. Remove the air bubbles, and adjust the headspace if needed. Wipe the rims of the jars with a clean, dampened paper towel; apply the preheated lids and the screw bands; and process the jars as indicated in the table that follows.

Apple Butter				
Recommended process time in a boiling-water canner				
		Process time at altitudes of		
Style of pack	**Jar size**	**0–1,000 ft**	**1,001–6,000 ft**	**Above 6,000 ft**
Hot	Half-pints or Pints	5 min	10 min	15 min
	Quarts	10	15	20

APPLE JUICE

QUALITY: Good apple juice is often made from a blend of apple varieties. If you're buying rather than making juice, be sure that it has been pressed within the past 24 hours.

PROCEDURE: Refrigerate the juice for 24 to 48 hours to let the solids settle out. Taking care not to shake the bottle, carefully pour off the clear juice and discard the sediment. For the clearest juice, strain it through a paper coffee filter or double layers of damp cheesecloth as you pour it into a pot. Heat the juice quickly, stirring occasionally, until it begins to boil. Immediately pour it into sterilized (see page 53) pint or quart jars or clean, hot half-gallon jars, leaving ¼ inch headspace. Wipe the rims of the jars with a clean, dampened paper towel; apply the preheated lids and the screw bands; and process the jars as indicated in the table that follows.

Apple Juice Recommended process time in a boiling-water canner				
		Process time at altitudes of		
Style of pack	**Jar size**	**0–1,000 ft**	**1,001–6,000 ft**	**Above 6,000 ft**
Hot	Pints or Quarts	5 min	10 min	15 min
	Half-gallons	10	15	20

APPLES—SLICED

QUANTITY: A quart jar holds about 2¾ pounds of sliced apples. You'll therefore need about 19 pounds of apples per 7-quart canner load or 12¼ pounds of apples per 9-pint canner load. A bushel of apples weighs 48 pounds and yields 16 to 19 quarts of apple slices.

QUALITY: Select crisp, juicy apples, and use a mix of sweet and tart, if possible. For the best result, hot-pack the apple slices.

PROCEDURE: Wash, peel, and core the apples. To keep them from browning as you work, slice them into water containing ascorbic acid (see page 48). Then drain the slices, weigh them, and put them into a pot. Add 1 pint of water or syrup (very light, light, or medium; see pages 96–98) per 5 pounds of sliced apples. Bring the liquid to a boil, and let it boil for 5 minutes, stirring occasionally to prevent burning. Fill hot jars with the hot slices and liquid, leaving ½ inch headspace. Remove the air bubbles, and adjust the headspace if needed. Wipe the rims of the jars with a clean, dampened paper towel, and apply the preheated lids and the screw bands. Process the jars in a boiling-water canner as indicated in the table that follows or in a dial- or weighted-gauge pressure canner as indicated in the tables on pages 134–135.

Sliced Apples Recommended process time in a boiling-water canner					
Style of pack	Jar size	**Process time at altitudes of**			
		0–1,000 ft	1,001– 3,000 ft	3,001– 6,000 ft	Above 6,000 ft
Hot	Pints or Quarts	20 min	25	30	35

APPLESAUCE

QUANTITY: You'll need about 3 pounds of apples to make a quart of applesauce, about 21 pounds for a canner load of 7 quarts, and about 13½ pounds for a canner load of 9 pints. A bushel of apples weighs 48 pounds and yields 14 to 19 quarts of applesauce.

QUALITY: Select sweet, juicy, crisp apples. For a tart flavor, add 1 to 2 pounds of tart apples to every 3 pounds of sweet.

PROCEDURE: Wash, peel, and core the apples. To keep them from browning as you work, slice them into water containing ascorbic acid (see page 48). Then drain the slices, put them into a pot, and add ½ cup of water. Stirring occasionally to prevent burning, heat the apples quickly until they are just tender (depending on the maturity, variety, and quantity, this will probably take 5 to 20 minutes). Press them through a sieve or food mill, or skip the pressing step if you prefer chunky applesauce. Taste the applesauce. If you'd like it sweeter, add as much as 2 tablespoons of sugar per quart. Reheat the sauce to a rolling boil. Fill hot jars with the hot sauce, leaving ½ inch headspace. Remove the air bubbles, and adjust the headspace if needed. Wipe the rims of the jars with a clean, dampened paper towel, and apply the preheated lids and the screw bands. Process the jars in a boiling-water canner as indicated in the table that follows or in a dial- or weighted-gauge pressure canner as indicated in the tables on pages 134–135.

Applesauce Recommended process time in a boiling-water canner					
Style of pack	Jar size	Process time at altitudes of			
		0– 1,000 ft	1,001– 3,000 ft	3,001– 6,000 ft	Above 6,000 ft
Hot	Pints	15 min	20	20	25
	Quarts	20	25	30	35

SPICED APPLE RINGS

12 lbs firm, tart apples, each no larger than 2½ inches across

12 cups sugar

6 cups water

1¼ cups white vinegar (5% acidity)

3 tbsp whole cloves

¾ cup red hot cinnamon candies, or 8 cinnamon sticks and 1 tsp red food coloring (optional)

YIELD: About 8 to 9 pints

PROCEDURE: Wash the apples. One at a time, peel each apple, slice it crosswise into ½-inch-thick slices, remove the core area (a melon baller works well for this purpose), and drop the slices into water containing ascorbic acid (see page 48). Combine the sugar, water, vinegar, cloves, and, if you like, the cinnamon candies or the cinnamon sticks and food coloring in a 6-quart saucepan. Stir, heat the mixture to boiling, and simmer the syrup for 3 minutes. Drain the apples, add them to the hot syrup, and cook them for 5 minutes. Fill hot jars, preferably wide-mouth ones, with the apple rings and hot syrup, leaving ½ inch headspace. Remove the air bubbles, and adjust the headspace if needed. Wipe the rims of the jars with a clean, dampened paper towel; apply the preheated lids and the screw bands; and process the jars as indicated in the table that follows.

Spiced Apple Rings				
Recommended process time in a boiling-water canner				
		Process time at altitudes of		
Style of pack	Jar size	0–1,000 ft	1,001–6,000 ft	Above 6,000 ft
Hot	Half-pints or Pints	10 min	15	20

SPICED CRAB APPLES

5 lbs crab apples

4½ cups apple cider vinegar (5% acidity)

3¾ cups water

7½ cups sugar

4 tsp whole cloves

4 sticks cinnamon

6 half-inch cubes fresh gingerroot

YIELD: About 9 pints

PROCEDURE: Wash the apples. Remove the calyx (the leafy bit) at the base of each apple, but leave the stem attached. Puncture the skin 4 times with an ice pick or toothpick. In a pot, mix the vinegar, water, and sugar, and bring the mixture to a boil. Add the spices, combined in a spice bag or tied in a small piece of cheesecloth. Using a blanching basket or sieve, immerse a third of the apples at a time in the boiling liquid for 2 minutes. Put the cooked apples and spice bag into a clean 1- or 2-gallon crock or bowl, and add the hot syrup. Cover the container, and let it stand overnight. Then remove the spice bag, drain the syrup into a large saucepan, and heat the syrup to boiling. Fill hot pint jars with the apples. Pour the hot syrup over the apples, leaving ½ inch headspace. Remove the air bubbles, and adjust the headspace if needed. Wipe the rims of the jars with a clean, dampened paper towel; apply the preheated lids and the screw bands; and process the jars as indicated in the table that follows.

Spiced Crab Apples					
Recommended process time in a boiling-water canner					
		Process time at altitudes of			
Style of pack	Jar size	0–1,000 ft	1,001–3,000 ft	3,001–6,000 ft	Above 6,000 ft
Hot	Pints	20 min	25	30	35

APRICOTS—HALVED OR SLICED

QUANTITY: About 2¼ pounds of apricots fill a quart jar, so you'll need about 16 pounds of fruit to fill 7 quart jars or about 10 pounds to fill 9 pint jars. A bushel of apricots weighs 50 pounds and yields 20 to 25 quarts.

QUALITY: Select firm, well-colored, mature fruit of ideal quality for eating fresh.

PROCEDURE: Hot-pack or raw-pack apricots according to the directions for peaches (see pages 121–122). If you prefer, you can leave the skins on, skipping the boiling-water dip; just be sure to wash the apricots well before proceeding.

BERRIES—WHOLE

You can hot-pack blueberries, currants, elderberries, gooseberries, or huckleberries, if you prefer, but you should raw-pack cane berries (blackberries, raspberries, or loganberries). Can the berries in juice, water, or syrup of the strength you prefer (see pages 96–98).

QUANTITY: About 1¾ pounds of berries fill a quart jar, so you'll need about 12 pounds to fill 7 quart jars or about 8 pounds to fill 9 pint jars. A 24-quart crate of berries weighs 36 pounds and yields 18 to 24 quarts.

QUALITY: Choose ripe, sweet berries with uniform color.

PROCEDURE: Wash 1 to 2 quarts of berries at a time. Drain, cap, and stem the berries, if needed. For gooseberries, snip off the stems and calyxes (the papery or leafy pieces enclosing the berries) with scissors. Bring the syrup, juice, or water to a boil, and add ½ cup of the hot liquid to each clean jar.

If you're hot-packing, use a blanching basket or sieve to heat the berries in boiling water for 30 seconds, let them drain, and then fill hot jars with the blanched berries.

If you're raw-packing, fill hot jars with raw berries, shaking them down gently.

Whether you're hot- or raw-packing the fruit, cover the berries with hot syrup, juice, or water, leaving ½ inch headspace. Remove the air bubbles, and adjust the headspace if needed. Wipe the rims of the jars with a clean, dampened paper towel, and apply the preheated lids and the screw bands. Process the jars in a boiling-water canner as indicated in the table that follows or in a dial- or weighted-gauge pressure canner as indicated in the tables on pages 134–135.

Whole Berries					
Recommended process time in a boiling-water canner					
		Process time at altitudes of			
Style of pack	Jar size	0–1,000 ft	1,001–3,000 ft	3,001–6,000 ft	Above 6,000 ft
Hot	Pints or Quarts	15 min	20	20	25
Raw	Pints	15	20	20	25
	Quarts	20	25	30	35

BERRY SYRUP

Juice from fresh or frozen blueberries, cherries, grapes, raspberries (black or red), or strawberries is easily made into a topping for use on ice cream, pastries, pancakes, and waffles.

YIELD: About 9 half-pints

PROCEDURE: Measure 6½ cups fresh or frozen berries of your choice. If the berries are fresh, wash, cap, and stem them as needed. Crush the berries in a saucepan. Heat the crushed fruit to boiling, and simmer it until soft (5 to 10 minutes). Drain the hot juice first through a colander and then through a jelly bag or double layer of cheesecloth. Discard the dry pulp. You should have about 4½ to 5 cups of juice. Combine the juice with 6¾ cups sugar in a large saucepan, bring the mixture to a boil while stirring, and simmer the syrup 1 minute. Remove the pan from the heat, skim off any foam, and fill hot half-pint or pint jars with the syrup, leaving ½ inch headspace. Remove the air bubbles, and adjust the headspace if needed. Wipe the rims of the jars with a clean, dampened paper towel; apply the preheated lids and the screw bands; and process the jars as indicated in the table that follows.

VARIATION: If you would like whole pieces of fruit in your syrup, reserve 1 to 2 cups of the fresh or frozen berries, and add them to the pan with the juice and sugar.

		Process time at altitudes of		
Style of pack	**Jar size**	**0–1,000 ft**	**1,001–6,000 ft**	**Above 6,000 ft**
Hot	Half-pints or Pints	10 min	15	20

Berry Syrup
Recommended process time in a boiling-water canner

CANTALOUPE PICKLES

The cantaloupes for these pickles should be full size, but the skins should be greenish, and the melons should be firm to the touch all over, even in the stem area. The pickles take 2 days to make.

5 lbs 1-inch cantaloupe cubes (from about 2 medium-size underripe cantaloupes)
1 tsp crushed red pepper flakes
2 one-inch-long cinnamon sticks
2 tsp ground cloves
1 tsp ground ginger
4½ cups cider vinegar (5% acidity)
2 cups water
1½ cups white sugar
1½ cups packed light brown sugar

YIELD: About 4 pints

PROCEDURE: Day One. Cut each cantaloupe into halves, and remove the seeds. Cut the halves into 1-inch-wide strips, and peel them. Cut the strips into 1-inch cubes. Weigh out 5 pounds of pieces, and put them in a large glass bowl. Put the red pepper flakes, cinnamon sticks, cloves, and ginger in a spice bag or small piece of cheesecloth, and tie the ends firmly. Combine the vinegar and water in a pot with a capacity of at least 4 quarts. Bring the liquid to a boil, then turn off the heat. Add the spice bag to the vinegar-water mixture, and let the spices steep for 5 minutes, stirring occasionally. Pour the hot vinegar solution with the spice bag over the melon pieces in the bowl. Cover the bowl with a food-grade plastic lid or plastic wrap, and let the bowl stand in the refrigerator for about 18 hours.

Day Two. Carefully drain off the vinegar solution into an 8- to 10-quart pot, and bring the liquid to a boil. Add the sugars, stir to dissolve them, then add the cantaloupe pieces. Bring the liquid back to a boil.

Lower the heat, and simmer until the cantaloupe pieces turn partially translucent (about 1 to 1¼ hours). With a slotted spoon, remove the cantaloupe pieces to a bowl. Cover the bowl, and set it aside. Bring the liquid remaining in the pot to a boil, and boil it for 5 minutes. Return the cantaloupe to the liquid, and bring the liquid back to a boil. Fill hot pint jars with the hot cantaloupe pieces, leaving 1 inch headspace. Carefully pour hot liquid over the cantaloupe pieces to cover them, leaving ½ inch headspace. Remove the air bubbles, and adjust the headspace if needed. Wipe the rims of the jars with a clean, dampened paper towel; apply the preheated lids and the screw bands; and process the jars as indicated in the table that follows.

Cantaloupe Pickles				
Recommended process time in a boiling-water canner				
			Process time at altitudes of	
Style of pack	Jar size	0–1,000 ft	1,001–6,000 ft	Above 6,000 ft
Hot	Pints	15 min	20	25

CANTALOUPE PICKLES, NO SUGAR ADDED

Just as in the preceding recipe, this one requires full-sized but greenish-skinned melons that are still firm, even at the stem end.

6 lbs of 1-inch cantaloupe cubes (from about 3 medium
underripe cantaloupes)
1 tsp crushed red pepper flakes
2 one-inch-long cinnamon sticks
2 tsp ground cloves
1 tsp ground ginger
4½ cups cider vinegar (5% acidity)
2 cups water
3 cups Splenda®

YIELD: About 4 pints

PROCEDURE: Follow the directions in the preceding recipe for "Cantaloupe Pickles," but weigh out 6 pounds of cantaloupe cubes instead of 5, and substitute the Splenda® for the sugar.

CHERRIES—WHOLE

This recipe works for both sweet cherries, such as Bing, and sour cherries, such as Montmorency. You may can cherries in water, juice (cherry, apple, or white grape), or sugar syrup in the strength you prefer (see pages 96–98).

QUANTITY: A quart jar holds about 2½ pounds of cherries. You'll therefore need about 17½ pounds of cherries to fill 7 quart jars or 11 pounds to fill 9 pint jars. A lug of cherries weighs 25 pounds and yields 8 to 12 quarts.

QUALITY: Select mature, glossy-skinned cherries of ideal quality for eating fresh or cooking.

PROCEDURE: Stem and wash the cherries, and pit them if you prefer. If you're pitting them, put them in water containing ascorbic acid (see page 48) as you work; this will keep the stem end of each from discoloring. If you're canning the cherries with their pits, prick the skin of each cherry twice, on opposite sides, with a clean needle; this will help keep the skin from splitting.

To hot-pack the cherries, combine them in a pot with ½ cup of water, juice, or syrup per quart of drained fruit. Bring the mixture to a boil, and fill hot jars with the cherries and their cooking liquid, leaving ½ inch headspace.

To raw-pack the cherries, pour ½ cup of hot water, juice, or syrup into each hot jar. Fill the jars with cherries, shaking them down gently. Add more hot liquid to cover them, leaving ½ inch headspace.

Whether you're hot- or raw-packing the fruit, remove the air bubbles, and adjust the headspace if needed. Wipe the rims of the jars with a clean, dampened paper towel, and apply the preheated lids and the screw bands. Process the jars in a boiling-water canner as indicated in the table that follows or in a dial- or weighted-gauge pressure canner as indicated in the tables on pages 134–135.

		Process time at altitudes of			
Style of pack	Jar size	0– 1,000 ft	1,001– 3,000 ft	3,001– 6,000 ft	Above 6,000 ft
Hot	Pints	15 min	20	20	25
	Quarts	20	25	30	35
Raw	Pints or Quarts	25	30	35	40

Whole Cherries
Recommended process time in a boiling-water canner

CRANBERRY-ORANGE CHUTNEY

Feel free to enhance this recipe with dry spices such as cloves, dry mustard, or cayenne pepper. Add spices to taste while the chutney simmers.

24 ounces fresh, whole cranberries
2 cups chopped white onions
2 cups golden raisins
1½ cups white sugar
1½ cups packed brown sugar
2 cups distilled white vinegar (5% acidity)
1 cup orange juice
4 tsp peeled, grated fresh gingerroot
3 one-inch-long cinnamon sticks

YIELD: About 8 half-pints

PROCEDURE: Rinse the cranberries well. Combine all the ingredients in a large pot, and bring the mixture to a boil over high heat. Reduce the heat, and simmer gently for 15 minutes or until the cranberries are tender, stirring often to prevent scorching. Remove and discard the cinnamon sticks. Fill hot half-pint jars with the hot chutney, leaving ½ inch headspace. Remove the air bubbles, and adjust the headspace if needed. Wipe the jar rims with a clean, dampened paper towel; apply the preheated lids and the screw bands; and process the jars as indicated in the table that follows.

Cranberry-Orange Chutney			
Recommended process time in a boiling-water canner			
		Process time at altitudes of	
Style of pack	Jar size	0–1,000 ft	1,001–6,000 ft	Above 6,000 ft
Hot	Half-pints	10 min	15	20

FIGS

Figs must always be acidified before they're canned in a boiling-water canner. The added acid protects them from the microorganism that causes botulism.

QUANTITY: A quart jar holds about 2½ pounds of figs. You'll therefore need about 16 pounds of figs to fill 7 quart jars or about 11 pounds to fill 9 pint jars.

QUALITY: Select figs that are just ripe—quite sweet but still firm and uncracked. The mature color will depend on the variety.

PROCEDURE: Wash and drain the figs, but do not peel or stem them. Lay the figs in a pan, cover them with water, bring the water to a boil, and boil them for 2 minutes. Drain the figs. Prepare a light syrup (see pages 96–98), and gently boil the figs in the syrup for 5 minutes. Add acid to hot jars: 2 tablespoons of bottled lemon juice per quart or 1 tablespoon per pint, or ½ teaspoon of citric acid per quart or ¼ teaspoon per pint. Fill the jars with the hot figs and syrup, leaving ½ inch headspace. Remove the air bubbles, and adjust the headspace if needed. Wipe the rims of the jars with a clean, dampened paper towel; apply the preheated lids and the screw bands; and process the jars as indicated in the table that follows.

		Figs			
		Recommended process time in a boiling-water canner			
		Process time at altitudes of			
Style of pack	**Jar size**	**0– 1,000 ft**	**1,001– 3,000 ft**	**3,001– 6,000 ft**	**Above 6,000 ft**
Hot	Pints	45 min	50	55	60
	Quarts	50	55	60	65

FRUIT PURÉES

This recipe should not be used with tomatoes, figs, cantaloupe or other melons, papaya, ripe mango, or coconut. For instructions on canning tomato purée, see "Tomato Juice," on pages 156–157 . For instructions on canning mango purée, see "Mango Sauce," on pages 118–119. **There are no home-canning recommendations available for pureed fig, melon, papaya, or coconut.**

PROCEDURE: Wash and drain the fruit that is to be puréed and canned; stem, peel, and pit the fruit as necessary. Measure the fruit and put it into a pot, crushing it slightly, if you prefer. Add 1 cup of hot water for each quart of fruit. Cook the fruit slowly, stirring frequently, until it is soft, and then press it through a sieve or food mill. Add sugar to taste, if you like. Then reheat the pulp to a boil or until any added sugar dissolves. Fill hot jars with the hot purée, leaving ¼ inch headspace. Remove the air bubbles, and adjust the headspace if needed. Wipe the rims of the jars with a clean, dampened paper towel, and apply the preheated lids and the screw bands. Process the jars in a boiling-water canner as indicated in the table that follows or in a dial- or weighted-gauge pressure canner as indicated in the tables on pages 134–135.

Fruit Purées Recommended process time in a boiling-water canner				
		Process time at altitudes of		
Style of pack	**Jar size**	**0–1,000 ft**	**1,001–6,000 ft**	**Above 6,000 ft**
Hot	Pints or Quarts	15 min	20	25

GRAPEFRUIT AND ORANGE SECTIONS

QUANTITY: A quart jar holds about 2 pounds of peeled orange or grapefruit sections. You'll therefore need about 15 pounds of fruit to fill 7 quart jars or about 13 pounds to fill 9 pint jars.

QUALITY: Select firm, mature, sweet fruit that is of ideal quality for eating fresh. Orange sections taste better if they are canned in the same jars with equal parts grapefruit sections. Grapefruit sections are good canned on their own, too. Pack the fruit in your choice of water, citrus juice, or syrup.

PROCEDURE: Wash and peel the fruit, and cut away any white tissue, which would cause bitterness in the canned fruit. If you want to can the fruit in syrup, prepare a very light, light, or medium syrup (see pages 96–98). Bring the syrup, water, or juice to a boil. Fill hot jars with the raw fruit sections and the hot liquid, leaving ½ inch headspace. Remove the air bubbles, and adjust the headspace if needed. Wipe the rims of the jars with a clean, dampened paper towel, and apply the preheated lids and the screw bands. Process the jars in a boiling-water canner as indicated in the table that follows or in a dial- or weighted-gauge pressure canner as indicated in the tables on pages 134–135.

Grapefruit and Orange Sections				
Recommended process time in a boiling-water canner				
Style of pack	Jar size	Process time at altitudes of		
		0–1,000 ft	1,001–6,000 ft	Above 6,000 ft
Raw	Pints or Quarts	10 min	15	20

GRAPE JUICE

QUANTITY: About 3½ pounds of grapes make enough juice to fill a quart jar. You'll therefore need about 24½ pounds of grapes to produce 7 quarts of juice or about 16 pounds of grapes to produce 9 pints. A lug of grapes weighs 26 pounds and yields 7 to 9 quarts of juice. The juice takes 2 to 3 days to make.

QUALITY: Select sweet, well-colored, firm, mature fruit of ideal quality for eating fresh or cooking.

PROCEDURE: Day One. Wash and stem the grapes. Put them in a pot, and add enough boiling water to cover them. Heat the grapes to a simmer, and then simmer them slowly until their skins are soft. Drain the juice through a dampened jelly bag or double layers of cheesecloth. Refrigerate the juice in a covered container for 24 to 48 hours.

Day Two or Three. Taking care not to shake the container, pour off the clear juice, leaving the sediment behind. For an even clearer product, strain the juice through a paper coffee filter. Then pour the juice into a pot, and, if you like, sweeten it to taste with sugar. Heat the juice, stirring, until the sugar is dissolved and the juice begins to boil. Immediately pour the juice into sterilized pint or quart jars or into hot half-gallon jars, leaving ¼ inch headspace. Wipe the rims of the jars with a clean, dampened paper towel; apply the preheated lids and the screw bands; and process the jars as indicated in the table that follows.

Grape Juice				
Recommended process time in a boiling-water canner				
		Process time at altitudes of		
Style of pack	Jar size	0–1,000 ft	1,001–6,000 ft	Above 6,000 ft
Hot	Pints or Quarts	5 min	10	15
	Half-gallons	10	15	20

GRAPES—WHOLE

QUANTITY: A quart jar holds about 2 pounds of whole grapes. You'll therefore need about 14 pounds of grapes to fill 7 quart jars or 9 pounds of grapes to fill 9 pint jars. A lug of grapes weighs 26 pounds and yields 12 to 14 quarts of canned whole grapes.

QUALITY: Choose tight-skinned, seedless grapes, preferably green ones, about 2 weeks before they reach optimal ripeness for eating fresh.

PROCEDURE: Stem, wash, and drain the grapes. Prepare very light or light syrup (see pages 96–98). If you're hot-packing the grapes, blanch them in boiling water for 30 seconds, then drain them. Fill hot jars with the blanched or raw grapes and the hot syrup, leaving 1 inch headspace. Remove the air bubbles, and adjust the headspace if needed. Wipe the rims of the jars with a clean, dampened paper towel; apply the preheated lids and the screw bands; and process the jars as indicated in the table that follows.

Whole Grapes					
Recommended process time in a boiling-water canner					
		Process time at altitudes of			
Style of pack	Jar size	0–1,000 ft	1,001–3,000 ft	3,001–6,000 ft	Above 6,000 ft
Hot	Pints or Quarts	10 min	15	15	20
Raw	Pints	15	20	20	25
	Quarts	20	25	30	35

MANGO SAUCE

Use slightly underripe or just-ripe mangoes for this recipe. **Green (underripe) mangoes irritate the skin of some people in the same way poison ivy does (they're in the same plant family), so if you're using green mangoes, wear plastic or rubber gloves while working with them, and avoid touching your face, lips, or eyes until you've washed all traces of raw mango from the gloves.**

To purée mangoes, wash and peel them, and cut out the pits. Cut the flesh into chunks. Whirl the chunks in a blender or food processor until the fruit is a smooth purée.

5½ cups mango purée
6 tbsp honey
4 tbsp bottled lemon juice
¾ cup sugar
2½ tsp ascorbic acid
⅛ tsp ground cinnamon
⅛ tsp ground nutmeg

YIELD: About 6 half-pints

PROCEDURE: Combine all the ingredients in a large pot. Place the pot over medium-high heat, and stir continuously until the mixture reaches 200°F. It will sputter as it heats, so be sure to wear gloves or oven mitts to avoid burning your skin. Fill hot half-pint jars with the hot sauce, leaving ¼ inch headspace. Remove the air bubbles, and adjust the headspace if needed. Wipe the rims of the jars with a clean, dampened paper towel; apply the preheated lids and the screw bands; and process the jars as indicated in the table that follows. To keep the sauce from discoloring, store the jars in a dark place, and use up the sauce within 6 months.

Mango Sauce				
Recommended process time in a boiling-water canner				
		Process time at altitudes of		
Style of pack	Jar size	0–1,000 ft	1,001–6,000 ft	Above 6,000 ft
Hot	Half-pints	15 min	20	25

MIXED FRUIT COCKTAIL

1½ lbs slightly underripe seedless green grapes

3 lbs ripe but firm peaches

3 lbs ripe but firm pears

3 cups sugar

4 cups water

1 ten-ounce jar maraschino cherries

YIELD: About 6 pints

PROCEDURE: Stem and wash the grapes, and keep them in water containing ascorbic acid (see page 48) while you prepare the other fruits. Dip the peaches in boiling water for 30 to 60 seconds to loosen their skins, then quickly dip the peaches in cold water, and slip off the skins. Halve and pit the peaches, cut them into ½-inch cubes, and put the cubes into the acidified water with the grapes. Peel, halve, and core the pears. Cut them into ½-inch cubes, and put the cubes in the acidified water with the grapes and peaches. Combine the sugar and water in a saucepan, and bring this syrup to a boil. Drain the mixed fruits. Put ½ cup hot syrup into each hot pint jar. Add a few cherries, and then gently fill each jar with the mixed fruits and more hot syrup, leaving ½ inch headspace. Remove the air bubbles, and adjust the headspace if needed. Wipe the rims of the jars with a clean, dampened paper towel; apply the preheated lids and the screw bands; and process the jars as indicated in the table that follows.

Mixed Fruit Cocktail Recommended process time in a boiling-water canner					
Style of pack	Jar size	Process time at altitudes of			
		0– 1,000 ft	1,001– 3,000 ft	3,001– 6,000 ft	Above 6,000 ft
Raw	Half-pints or Pints	20 min	25	30	35

NECTARINES—HALVED OR SLICED

QUANTITY: A quart jar holds about 2½ pounds of halved or sliced nectarines. You'll therefore need about 17½ pounds of nectarines to fill 7 quart jars or about 11 pounds to fill 9 pint jars. A bushel of nectarines weighs 48 pounds and yields 16 to 24 quarts.

QUALITY: Choose ripe, mature fruit of ideal quality for eating fresh or cooking.

PROCEDURE: Use the directions that follow for peaches, but do not dip the nectarines in hot water or remove their skins; just wash the nectarines before slicing them. Either the hot-pack or raw-pack method is suitable.

PEACHES—HALVED OR SLICED

You can either hot-pack or raw-pack peaches, but hot-packing produces better results. Can your peaches in syrup, water, apple juice, or grape juice.

QUANTITY: A quart jar holds about 2½ pounds of halved or sliced peaches. You'll therefore need about 17½ pounds of peaches to fill 7 quart jars or about 11 pounds to fill 9 pint jars. A bushel of peaches weighs 48 pounds and yields 16 to 24 quarts.

QUALITY: Choose ripe, mature fruit of ideal quality for eating fresh or cooking.

PROCEDURE: Dip the peaches in boiling water for 30 to 60 seconds, just until their skins loosen. Then quickly dip them in cold water, and slip off the skins. Halve the peaches, remove their pits, and slice them, if you prefer.

As you work, keep the cut fruit in water containing ascorbic acid (see page 48) to prevent browning. If you want to can the peaches in syrup, prepare very light, light, or medium syrup (see pages 96–98).

To hot-pack the peaches, put the syrup, water, or juice in a pot; add the drained peaches; and bring the contents to a boil.

If you're raw-packing, just heat the syrup, water, or juice to a boil.

Whether you are hot- or raw-packing, fill hot jars with the hot or raw peaches; place them cut-side down if you're canning halves. Add the hot liquid, leaving ½ inch headspace. Remove the air bubbles, and adjust the headspace if needed. Wipe the rims of the jars with a clean, dampened paper towel, and apply the preheated lids and the screw bands. Process the jars in a boiling-water canner as indicated in the table that follows or in a dial- or weighted-gauge pressure canner as indicated in the tables on pages 134–135.

Halved or Sliced Peaches					
Recommended process time in a boiling-water canner					
		Process time at altitudes of			
Style of pack	Jar size	0–1,000 ft	1,001–3,000 ft	3,001–6,000 ft	Above 6,000 ft
Hot	Pints	20 min	25	30	35
	Quarts	25	30	35	40
Raw	Pints	25	30	35	40
	Quarts	30	35	40	45

PEARS—HALVED

Hot-packing, as described in this recipe, makes for the best canned pears. Can your pears in syrup, water, apple juice, or grape juice.

QUANTITY: A quart jar holds about 2½ pounds of pear halves. You'll therefore need about 17½ pounds of pears to fill 7 quart jars or about 11 pounds to fill 9 pint jars. A bushel of pears weighs 50 pounds and yields 16 to 25 quarts of pear halves.

QUALITY: Choose ripe, mature fruit of ideal quality for eating fresh or cooking.

PROCEDURE: Wash and peel the pears. Cut them in half lengthwise, and remove the cores; a melon baller or metal measuring spoon works well for this purpose. To prevent browning, keep the cut pears in water containing ascorbic acid (see page 48) while you work. If you want to can the pears in syrup, prepare a very light, light, or medium syrup (see pages 96–98). Pour the syrup, juice, or water into a pot. Add the drained pears, and bring the contents to a boil. Boil the pears for 5 minutes. Fill hot jars with the hot pears and cooking liquid, leaving ½ inch headspace. Remove the air bubbles, and adjust the headspace if needed. Wipe the jar rims with a clean, dampened paper towel, and apply the preheated lids and the screw bands. Process the jars in a boiling-water canner as indicated in the table that follows or in a dial- or weighted-gauge pressure canner as indicated in the tables on pages 134–135.

Halved Pears					
Recommended process time in a boiling-water canner					
		Process time at altitudes of			
Style of pack	Jar size	0–1,000 ft	1,001–3,000 ft	3,001–6,000 ft	Above 6,000 ft
Hot	Pints	20 min	25	30	35
	Quarts	25	30	35	40

PEARS, ASIAN— HALVED OR SLICED

To prevent botulism, home-canned Asian pears must always be acidified before being canned in a boiling-water canner. For best quality, the pears should be hot-packed. Can Asian pears in syrup, water, apple juice, or white grape juice.

QUANTITY: A quart jar holds about 2½ pounds of halved or sliced Asian pears. You'll therefore need about 17 to 19 pounds of Asian pears to fill 7 quart jars or 11 to 13 pounds to fill 9 pint jars.

QUALITY: Choose ripe, mature fruit of ideal quality for eating fresh or cooking.

PROCEDURE: Wash and peel the pears. Halve them lengthwise, and remove the cores. Slice the pears, if you like. To prevent discoloration, keep the cut pears in water containing ascorbic acid (see page 48) while you work. If you want to can the pears in syrup, prepare a very light, light, or medium syrup (see pages 96–98). Drain the pears; put them into a pot with the syrup, juice, or water; and bring the contents to a boil. Boil the pears for 5 minutes. To acidify the pears, put bottled lemon juice in each hot jar—1 tablespoon per pint or 2 tablespoons per quart. Fill the jars with the hot fruit, and cover the fruit with the boiling cooking liquid, leaving ½ inch headspace. Remove the air bubbles, and adjust the headspace if needed. Wipe the rims of the jars with a clean, dampened paper towel; apply the preheated lids and the screw bands; and process the jars as indicated in the table that follows.

Halved or Sliced Asian Pears					
Recommended process time in a boiling-water canner					
Style of pack	Jar size	Process time at altitudes of			
		0–1,000 ft	1,001–3,000 ft	3,001–6,000 ft	Above 6,000 ft
Hot	Pints	20 min	25	30	35
	Quarts	25	30	35	40

PINEAPPLE

Pineapple may be canned in water; syrup; or pineapple, apple, or white-grape juice.

QUANTITY: A quart jar holds about 3 pounds of sliced or cubed pineapple. You'll therefore need about 21 pounds of pineapples to fill 7 quart jars or 13 pounds to fill 9 pint jars.

QUALITY: Select ripe but firm pineapples.

PROCEDURE: Wash the pineapples, peel them, and cut away their "eyes" and tough, fibrous centers. Slice or cube the flesh. If you want to can the pineapple in syrup, make a very light, light, or medium syrup (see pages 96–98). In a pot, combine the pineapple with the syrup, water, or juice, and simmer for 10 minutes. Fill hot jars with the hot fruit and cooking liquid, leaving ½ inch headspace. Remove the air bubbles, and adjust the headspace if needed. Wipe the rims of the jars with a clean, dampened paper towel; apply the preheated lids and the screw bands; and process the jars as indicated in the table that follows.

		Process time at altitudes of			
Style of pack	**Jar size**	**0– 1,000 ft**	**1,001– 3,000 ft**	**3,001– 6,000 ft**	**Above 6,000 ft**
Hot	Pints	15 min	20	20	25
	Quarts	20	25	30	35

Pineapple
Recommended process time in a boiling-water canner

PLUMS—HALVED OR WHOLE

You can put up plums either whole or, if they're a freestone variety, halved and pitted. Hot-pack or raw-pack the fruit, as you prefer, in either water or syrup.

QUANTITY: A quart jar holds about 2 pounds of plums. You'll therefore need about 14 pounds of plums to fill 7 quart jars or 9 pounds to fill 9 pint jars. A bushel of plums weighs 56 pounds and yields 22 to 36 quarts.

QUALITY: Select deeply colored, mature fruit of ideal quality for eating fresh or cooking.

PROCEDURE: Stem and wash the plums. If you're canning them whole, use a fork to prick each plum on opposite sides to keep the skin from splitting. Otherwise, halve and pit the plums. If you're using syrup, make it very light, light, or medium (see pages 96–98).

If you're hot-packing, put the plums in a pot with hot water or hot syrup, bring the contents to a boil, boil the plums for 2 minutes, and then cover the pan and let it stand for 20 to 30 minutes. Fill hot jars with the plums and cooking liquid.

If you're raw-packing, fill hot jars with the raw plums, packing them firmly, and cover them with hot water or syrup.

Whether you're hot- or raw-packing, leave ½ inch headspace. Remove the air bubbles, and adjust the headspace if needed. Wipe the rims of the jars with a clean, dampened paper towel, and apply the preheated lids and the screw bands. Process the jars in a boiling-water canner as indicated in the table that follows or in a dial- or weighted-gauge pressure canner as indicated in the tables on pages 134–135.

Halved or Whole Plums Recommended process time in a boiling-water canner					
		Process time at altitudes of			
Style of pack	**Jar size**	**0– 1,000 ft**	**1,001– 3,000 ft**	**3,001– 6,000 ft**	**Above 6,000 ft**
Hot or Raw	Pints	20 min	25	30	35
	Quarts	25	30	35	40

PIE FILLINGS

The pie fillings in this section are made with Clear Jel®, a chemically modified cornstarch that produces sauce of an excellent consistency even after canning and baking. Other available starches break down when used in pie fillings, causing the sauce to be runny.

Clear Jel® is available through only a few outlets, none of them grocery stores. Before you plan to make these pie fillings, find out where you can buy Clear Jel®. Your local Cooperative Extension office may be able to help you locate a source.

A quart jar holds enough filling to make a single 8- to 9-inch pie. You could also use the canned fruit as a topping for pastry or other desserts.

Because the variety of fruit you can will affect the flavor of your pie, you might first prepare just 1 quart and make a pie with it. Then adjust the sugar and spices in the recipe to suit your personal preferences. But don't reduce the amount of lemon juice; the acid in lemon juice preserves the safety and quality of the fillings.

APPLE PIE FILLING

	Quantities of ingredients needed for:	
	1 Quart	**7 Quarts**
Blanched, sliced, fresh apples	3½ cups	6 quarts
Granulated sugar	¾ cup + 2 tbsp	5½ cups
Clear Jel®	¼ cup	1½ cups
Cinnamon	½ tsp	1 tbsp
Cold water	½ cup	2½ cups
Apple juice	¾ cup	5 cups
Nutmeg (optional)	¼ tsp	1 tsp
Yellow food coloring (optional)	1 drop	7 drops
Bottled lemon juice	2 tbsp	¾ cup

QUALITY: Use firm, crisp, fresh apples that will hold up well in cooking. Suitable varieties include Stayman, Golden Delicious, and Rome. If your apples lack tartness, use an additional ¼ cup lemon juice for every 6 quarts of sliced apples.

YIELD: 1 quart or 7 quarts

PROCEDURE: Wash, peel, and core the apples, and slice them into ½-inch-thick slices. While you work, keep the slices in water containing ascorbic acid to prevent browning (see page 48). Then drain the slices and blanch them, 6 cups at a time, in 1 gallon of boiling water. Boil each batch for 1 minute after the water returns to a boil. Drain the apples, and keep them hot in a covered bowl or pot. In a large pot, combine the sugar, Clear Jel®, and cinnamon with the water, apple juice, and, if you like, nutmeg, food coloring, or both. Stirring, cook the mixture over medium-high heat until it thickens and begins to bubble. Add the lemon juice, and boil 1 minute, stirring constantly. Fold in the drained apple slices, and immediately fill hot jars with the mixture, leaving 1 inch headspace. Remove the air bubbles, and adjust the headspace if needed. Wipe the rims of the jars with a clean, dampened paper towel; apply the preheated lids and the screw bands; and process the jars immediately as indicated in the table on the next page.

Apple Pie Filling					
Recommended process time in a boiling-water canner					
		Process time at altitudes of			
Style of pack	Jar size	0–1,000 ft	1,001–3,000 ft	3,001–6,000 ft	Above 6,000 ft
Hot	Pints or Quarts	25 min	30	35	40

BLUEBERRY PIE FILLING

Quantities of Ingredients Needed For:		
	1 QUART	7 QUARTS
Fresh or thawed blueberries	3½ cups	6 quarts
Granulated sugar	¾ cup + 2 tbsp	6 cups
Clear Jel®	¼ cup + 1 tbsp	2¼ cups
Cold water	1 cup	7 cups
Blue food coloring (optional)	3 drops	20 drops
Red food coloring (optional)	1 drop	7 drops
Bottled lemon juice	3 tbsp	½ cup

QUALITY: Select fresh, ripe, firm blueberries.

YIELD: 1 quart or 7 quarts

PROCEDURE: Wash and drain the blueberries. Blanch 6 cups at a time in 1 gallon of boiling water; boil each batch for 1 minute after the water returns to a boil. Drain the berries, and keep them hot in a covered bowl or pot. Combine the sugar and Clear Jel® in a large pot. Stir. Add the water and, if you like, the food coloring. Continue stirring as you cook the mixture over medium-high heatuntil it thickens and begins to bubble. Add the lemon juice, and boil 1 minute, stirring constantly. Fold in the drained berries, andimmediately fill hot jars with the mixture, leaving 1 inch headspace. Remove the air bubbles, and adjust the headspace if needed. Wipe the rims of the jars with a clean, dampened paper towel; apply the preheated lids and the screw bands; and process the jars immediately as indicated in the table on the next page.

VARIATION: To use this recipe with frozen blueberries, first wash off any added sugar while the fruit is still frozen. Then let the fruit thaw, collect and measure the juice, and use the juice to replace some of the water in the recipe. Don't blanch the berries. Use only ¼ cup of Clear Jel® per quart or 1¾ cups of Clear Jel® per 7 quarts.

Blueberry Pie Filling Recommended process time in a boiling-water canner					
		Process time at altitudes of			
Style of pack	**Jar size**	**0–1,000 ft**	**1,001–3,000 ft**	**3,001–6,000 ft**	**Above 6,000 ft**
Hot	Pints or Quarts	30 min	35	40	45

CHERRY PIE FILLING

Quantities of ingredients needed for:	1 Quart	7 Quarts
Fresh or thawed sour cherries	3⅓ cups	6 quarts
Granulated sugar	1 cup	7 cups
Clear Jel®	¼ cup + 1 tbsp	1¾ cups
Cold water	1⅓ cups	9⅓ cups
Cinnamon (optional)	⅛ tsp	1 tsp
Almond extract (optional)	¼ tsp	2 tsp
Red food coloring (optional)	6 drops	¼ tsp
Bottled lemon juice	1 tbsp + 1 tsp	½ cup

QUALITY: Select fresh cherries that are very ripe but still firm.

YIELD: 1 quart or 7 quarts

PROCEDURE: Rinse and pit the cherries. To keep them from browning at the stem end, drop the pitted cherries into water containing ascorbic acid (see page 48). Blanch the cherries, 6 cups at a time, in 1 gallon of boiling water. Boil each batch for 1 minute after the water returns to a boil. Drain the cherries, and keep them hot in a covered bowl or pot. In a large pot, stir together the sugar and Clear Jel®.

Add the water and, if you like, the cinnamon, almond extract, food coloring, or any combination of these. Stirring, cook the mixture over medium-high heat until it thickens and begins to bubble. Add the lemon juice, and boil 1 minute, stirring constantly. Fold in the drained cherries, and immediately fill hot jars with the mixture, leaving 1 inch headspace. Remove the air bubbles, and adjust the headspace if needed. Wipe the rims of the jars with a clean, dampened paper towel; apply the preheated lids and the screw bands; and process the jars immediately as indicated in the table that follows.

Cherry Pie Filling Recommended process time in a boiling-water canner					
Style of pack	Jar size	Process time at altitudes of			
		0–1,000 ft	1,001–3,000 ft	3,001–6,000 ft	Above 6,000 ft
Hot	Pints or Quarts	30 min	35	40	45

PEACH PIE FILLING

Quantities of ingredients needed for:		
	1 Quart	7 Quarts
Sliced fresh peaches	3½ cups	6 quarts
Granulated sugar	1 cup	7 cups
Clear Jel®	¼ cup + 1 tbsp	2 cups + 3 tbsp
Cold water	¾ cup	5¼ cups
Cinnamon (optional)	⅛ tsp	1 tsp
Almond extract (optional)	⅛ tsp	1 tsp
Bottled lemon juice	¼ cup	1¾ cups

QUALITY: Select fresh peaches that are ripe but still firm. Red Haven, Redskin, and Sun High are some suitable varieties.

YIELD: 1 quart or 7 quarts

PROCEDURE: Submerge the peaches in boiling water for 30 to 60 seconds to loosen their skins, then dip the peaches in cold water, and slip off the skins. Slice the peaches into ½-inch-thick slices, and keep them in water containing ascorbic acid (see page 48) while you work. Drain the slices, then blanch them, 6 cups at a time, in 1 gallon of boiling water. Boil each batch for 1 minute after the water returns to a boil. Drain the slices, and keep them hot in a covered bowl or pot. In a large pot, combine the sugar, Clear Jel®, water, and, if you like, cinnamon or almond extract or both. Stirring, cook the mixture over medium-high heat until it thickens and begins to bubble. Add the lemon juice, and boil the sauce 1 minute more, stirring constantly. Fold in the peach slices, and heat the mixture 3 minutes more. Immediately fill hot jars with the mixture, leaving 1 inch headspace. Remove the air bubbles, and adjust the headspace if needed. Wipe the rims of the jars with a clean, dampened paper towel; apply the preheated lids and the screw bands; and process the jars immediately as indicated in the table that follows.

VARIATION: To use this recipe with frozen peaches, first wash off any added sugar while the fruit is still frozen. Then let the fruit thaw, collect and measure the juice, and use the juice to replace some of the water in the recipe. Don't blanch the peaches. Use only ¼ cup of Clear Jel® for each quart of filling or 1¾ cups of Clear Jel® for 7 quarts.

Peach Pie Filling
Recommended process time in a boiling-water canner

Style of pack	Jar size	Process time at altitudes of			
		0–1,000 ft	1,001–3,000 ft	3,001–6,000 ft	Above 6,000 ft
Hot	Pints or Quarts	30 min	35	40	45

Process times for some acid foods in a dial-gauge pressure canner

Type of fruit	Style of pack	Jar size	Process time (min)	Canner pressure (PSI) at altitudes of			
				0–2,000 ft	2,001–4,000 ft	4,001–6,000 ft	6,001–8,000 ft
Apples, sliced	Hot	Pints or Quarts	8	6 lbs	7 lbs	8 lbs	9 lbs
Applesauce	Hot	Pints	8	6	7	8	9
	Hot	Quarts	10	6	7	8	9
Berries, whole	Hot	Pints or Quarts	8	6	7	8	9
	Raw	Pints	8	6	7	8	9
	Raw	Quarts	10	6	7	8	9
Cherries, sour or sweet	Hot	Pints	8	6	7	8	9
	Hot	Quarts	10	6	7	8	9
	Raw	Pints or Quarts	10	6	7	8	9
Fruit purees	Hot	Pints or Quarts	8	6	7	8	9
Grapefruit and orange sections	Hot	Pints or Quarts	8	6	7	8	9
	Raw	Pints	8	6	7	8	9
	Raw	Quarts	10	6	7	8	9
Peaches, apricots, or nectarines	Hot or Raw	Pints or Quarts	10	6	7	8	9
Pears	Hot	Pints or Quarts	10	6	7	8	9
Plums	Hot or Raw	Pints or Quarts	10	6	7	8	9
Rhubarb	Hot	Pints or Quarts	8	6	7	8	9

Process times for some acid foods in a weighted-gauge pressure canner

Type of fruit	Style of pack	Jar size	Process time (min)	Canner pressure (PSI) at altitudes of	
				0–1,000 ft	Above 1,000 ft
Apples, sliced	Hot	Pints or Quarts	8	5 lbs	10 lbs
Applesauce	Hot	Pints	8	5	10
	Hot	Quarts	10	5	10
Berries, whole	Hot	Pints or Quarts	8	5	10
	Raw	Pints	8	5	10
	Raw	Quarts	10	5	10
Cherries, sour or sweet	Hot	Pints	8	5	10
	Hot	Quarts	10	5	10
	Raw	Pints or Quarts	10	5	10
Fruit purees	Hot	Pints or Quarts	8	5	10
Grapefruit and orange sections	Hot	Pints or Quarts	8	5	10
	Raw	Pints	8	5	10
	Raw	Quarts	10	5	10
Peaches, apricots, or nectarines	Hot or Raw	Pints or Quarts	10	5	10
Pears	Hot	Pints or Quarts	10	5	10
Plums	Hot or Raw	Pints or Quarts	10	5	10
Rhubarb	Hot	Pints or Quarts	8	5	10

JAMS & JELLIES

PREPARING SWEET SPREADS

Sweet spreads are a class of foods with many textures, flavors, and colors. They all consist of fruits preserved mostly by means of sugar, and they are thickened or gelled to some extent.

- **Fruit jelly** *is a semisolid mixture of fruit juice and sugar that is clear and firm enough to hold its shape.*

- **Jam** *also will hold its shape, but it is less firm than jelly. Jam is made from crushed or chopped fruits and sugar.*

- **Conserves** *are jams made from a mixture of fruits. This term is used especially when a jam includes citrus fruits, nuts, raisins, or coconut.*

- **Preserves** *are made of small, whole fruits or uniform-size pieces of fruit in a clear, thick, slightly jellied syrup.*

- **Marmalades** *are soft, transparent jellies with small pieces of fruit or citrus peel evenly suspended throughout.*

- **Fruit butters** *are made from fruit pulp cooked with sugar until thickened to a spreadable consistency.*

INGREDIENTS

For proper texture, gelled fruit products require the correct combination of fruit, pectin, acid, and sugar. The fruit gives each spread its unique flavor and color. The fruit also supplies the water to dissolve the rest of the necessary ingredients and furnishes some or all of the pectin and acid. Good-quality, flavorful fruits make the best gelled products.

Pectins are substances in fruits that form a gel if they are in the right combination with acid and sugar. All fruits contain some pectin. Apples, crab apples, gooseberries, and some plums and grapes usually contain enough natural pectin to form a gel. Other fruits, such as strawberries and cherries, contain little pectin and must be combined with other fruits high in pectin or with commercial pectin products to form strong gels. Because the pectin level declines as fruit becomes fully ripe, a quarter of the fruit used in making jellies without added pectin should be slightly underripe.

The proper level of acidity is critical to gel formation. If there is too little acid, the gel will never set; if there is too much acid, the gel will lose liquid, or "weep." When you're using fruits that are low in acid, add lemon juice or another acid ingredient as directed. Commercial pectin products contain acids that help to ensure gelling.

Sugar helps preserve sweet spreads, contributes flavor, and aids in gelling. Cane and beet sugar are the usual sources of sugar for jelly or jam. Too little sugar prevents gelling and may allow yeasts and molds to grow.

JUICE ALERT

Commercially frozen and canned juices are usually low in natural pectins, so sweet spreads made with these juices will have a soft texture.

Corn syrup or honey can be used to replace part of the sugar, but too much will mask the flavor of the fruit and alter the gel structure. It's better to use tested recipes that replace sugar with honey or corn syrup rather than to reduce the amount of sugar in conventional recipes.

JAMS AND JELLIES WITH REDUCED SUGAR

Jellies and jams that contain modified pectin (see the following paragraph), gelatin, or gums can be made with noncaloric sweeteners. Low-sugar jams can also be made with concentrated fruit pulp.

Two types of **modified pectin** are available for home use. One gels with ⅓ less sugar than regular pectin. The other type is **low-methoxyl pectin,** which requires a source of calcium for gelling. To prevent spoilage, jars containing either of these products may need to be processed longer in a boiling-water canner. Recipes and processing times provided with each modified-pectin product should be followed carefully. Spoilage could result if you alter the proportions of acids and fruits.

Softly gelled refrigerator fruit spreads can also be made with gelatin and sugar substitutes. Such products spoil at room temperature and so should be kept in the refrigerator and eaten within a month.

PREVENTING SPOILAGE

Even though sugar helps preserve jellies and jams, molds can grow on their surface. Research now shows that the mold people often scrape off the surface of jellies may not be harmless. Mycotoxins, which are known to cause cancer in animals, have been found in some jars of jelly with surface mold growth (the effects of mycotoxins on humans are still being researched). And wax seals are no longer recommended for any sweet spreads because they pose a risk of mold contamination.

To prevent both the growth of molds and the loss of good flavor or color, pour your jelly syrup or hot jam into Mason jars that have been sterilized as described on pages 52-53. Leave ¼ inch headspace; cap the jars with preheated, self-sealing lids and screw bands; and process the jars for 5 minutes in a boiling-water canner. At an elevation of 1,000 feet or higher, add 1 minute of processing time per 1,000 feet above sea level.

You can use unsterilized jars if you prefer, but if you do, process the jars for 10 minutes. There is some chance that the added 5 minutes of processing could weaken the gel, especially with fruits low in pectin, so the use of sterilized jars is preferable.

METHODS OF MAKING JAMS AND JELLIES

There are 2 basic methods of making jams and jellies. The traditional method, which requires no added pectin, works best with fruits that are naturally high in pectin. These include apples, crab apples, gooseberries, some plums, and grapes. The other method, which requires the use of commercial liquid or powdered pectin, is quicker.

The gelling ability of various pectins differs. To make uniformly gelled products, be sure to add the quantity of commercial pectin to a specific fruit as instructed on each package.

A good gel depends on the right amount of cooking. Undercooked jams and jellies won't set. Overcooking can break down pectin and also prevent proper gelling. If you're using commercial pectin, time the boiling exactly as instructed on the package. If you're using the traditional method, be prepared to test for signs of gelling in jelly using a thermometer or the sheet or spoon test (page 143) and in jam using a thermometer or the refrigerator test (page 145).

Whether or not you're adding commercial pectin, make only a single batch of jam or jelly at a time according to the recipe. Increasing the quantities could result in a soft gel.

Stir constantly while cooking sweet preserves to prevent them from scalding. Recipes for sweet preserves have been developed for specific jar sizes. Jellies put into larger jars may turn out too soft.

MAKING JELLY WITHOUT ADDED PECTIN

Jelly is made from fruit juice. To make jelly without added pectin, collect juice from firm fruits that are naturally high in pectin (apples, crab apples, gooseberries, some plums, and grapes). Use 3 parts ripe fruit to 1 part underripe. One pound of fruit should yield at least 1 cup of clear juice.

Do not use commercially canned or frozen fruit juices, because their pectin content is too low.

To render the juice, first wash the fruit thoroughly. Crush berries or other soft fruit; cut firmer fruit into small pieces. Put the fruit into a pot. You can include peels and cores for a higher pectin content, if you like. Add water, if directed to do so in the table below. Bring the fruit and any water to a boil. Then simmer the fruit for the time listed in the table, stirring constantly to prevent scorching.

Extracting and Preparing Juice to Make Jelly					
	Water (in cups) to be added per pound of fruit	Minutes to simmer fruit before extracting juice	Ingredients to be added to each cup of strained juice		Yield of jelly (in half-pints) from 4 cups of juice
			Sugar (cups)	Lemon juice (tsp)	
Apples	1	20 to 25	¾	1½ (optional)	4 to 5
Blackberries	None or ¼	5 to 10	¾ to 1	None	7 to 8
Crab apples	1	20 to 25	1	None	4 to 5
Grapes	None or ¼	5 to 10	¾ to 1	None	8 to 9
Plums	½	15 to 20	¾	None	8 to 9

When the fruit is tender, strain it first through a colander and then through either a double layer of cheesecloth laid in a colander or a jelly bag suspended from a stand. Let the juice drip into a suitable container. Don't press or squeeze the bag or cheesecloth; doing so will result in cloudy jelly.

Measure the juice. Using no more than 8 cups at a time, combine the juice with the amounts of sugar and lemon juice indicated in the table. Heat the mixture to boiling, stirring until the sugar is dissolved. Boil the syrup over high heat to the gelling point.

Test the jelly for doneness with either of the following methods:

TEMPERATURE TEST: Using an accurate thermometer as your guide, boil the mixture until it reaches the temperature specified for your altitude in the table that follows.

Gelling Temperatures at Various Altitudes								
Sea level	1,000 ft	2,000 ft	3,000 ft	4,000 ft	5,000 ft	6,000 ft	7,000 ft	8,000 ft
220°F	218°F	216°F	214°F	212°F	211°F	209°F	207°F	205°F

SHEET OR SPOON TEST: Dip a cool metal spoon into the boiling syrup. Raise the spoon about 12 inches above the pan and out of the steam. Turn the spoon so the liquid runs off the side. The jelly is done when the syrup forms 2 drops that flow together and "sheet," or hang, off the edge of the spoon, as shown in the illustration.

When the jelly is done, immediately remove the pot from the heat, and skim off any foam. Quickly ladle the jelly through a wide-mouth funnel into sterilized pint or half-pint jars (see page 53), leaving ¼ inch headspace. Wipe the rims of the jars with a clean, dampened paper towel before applying the preheated lids and the screw bands. Then process as directed on page 147.

MAKING JAM WITHOUT ADDED PECTIN

For best flavor, use fruit that is fully ripe but not overripe. Wash and rinse the fruit thoroughly, but don't soak it. Stem, skin, and pit the fruit, as needed. Cut the flesh into pieces, and crush it. If you're using seedy berries, press them through a sieve or food mill, if you prefer. Measure out the quantity of crushed fruit specified in the table below, and put the fruit in a large pot.

FOAMING AT THE POT?

To reduce foaming when you're cooking your jelly or jam, you can add half a teaspoon of butter or margarine to the pot. This could, however, cause an off flavor if you store your jelly or jam for a long time.

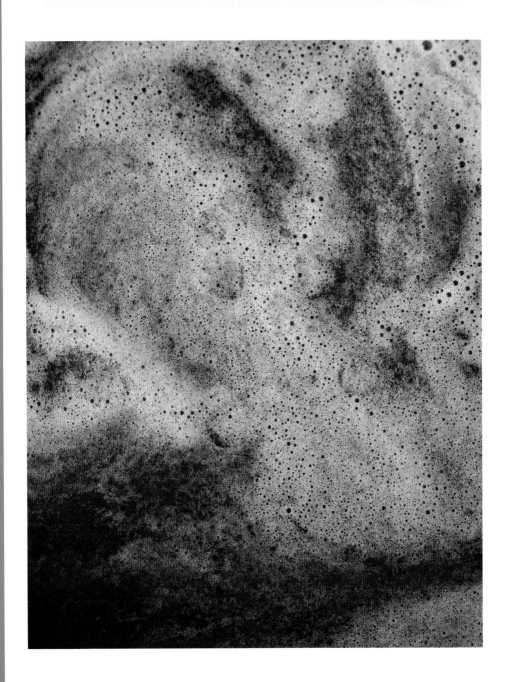

Formulas for Jams without Added Pectin				
Fruit	Crushed fruit (cups)	Sugar (cups)	Lemon juice (tbsp)	Yield (half-pints)
Apricots	4 to 4½	4	2	5 to 6
Berries*	4	4	0	3 to 4
Peaches	5½ to 6	4 to 5	2	6 to 7

* Includes blackberries, boysenberries, dewberries, gooseberries, loganberries, raspberries, and strawberries

Add the amount of sugar (and lemon juice, if called for) specified in the table, and bring the mixture to a boil while stirring rapidly and constantly. Continue to boil the mixture until it thickens. Remember that the jam will thicken more as it cools.

Use either of the following tests to determine if the jam is ready:

TEMPERATURE TEST: Using an accurate thermometer as your guide, boil the mixture until it reaches the right temperature for your altitude, as specified in the table on page 143.

REFRIGERATOR TEST: Remove the pot from the heat. Spoon a little of the hot jam onto a cold plate, and then put the plate in the freezer for a few minutes. If the mixture gels, it is ready to be put in jars.

When the jam is ready, remove the pot from the heat, if you haven't already. Quickly skim off any foam. Ladle the jam through a wide-mouth funnel into sterilized pint or half-pint jars, leaving ¼ inch headspace. Wipe the rims of the jars with a clean, dampened paper towel before attaching the preheated lids and the screw bands. Then process as directed on page 147.

MAKING JELLIES AND JAMS WITH ADDED PECTIN

Jelly or jam made with commercially prepared pectin—powdered or liquid—needs less cooking than traditional jam or jelly and usually requires less fruit for the same yield. Sweet spreads made with added pectin may have a fresher fruit flavor, too. And, because pectin is being added, they can be made from commercially canned or frozen fruit juice or from fresh fruit or juice.

Packaged pectin must be bought fresh every year. Old pectin can cause weak gels.

The preparation method for jellies and jams with added pectin varies somewhat depending on the type of pectin. Complete directions for a variety of fruits are provided in the pectin package. These recipes include:

JELLIES: Apple, crab apple, blackberry, boysenberry, currant, dewberry, elderberry, grape, loganberry, mayhaw, mint, peach, plum, black or red raspberry, rhubarb, and strawberry.

JAMS: Apricot, blackberry, blueberry, boysenberry, cherry, currant, dewberry, fig, gooseberry, grape, loganberry, orange marmalade, peach, pear, plum, black or red raspberry, rhubarb, strawberry, spiced tomato, and youngberry.

PROCESSING FULL-SUGAR JAM OR JELLY

Can your full-sugar jams and jellies in sterilized Mason jars (see page 53) capped with preheated, self-sealing lids and screw bands. Process the jars in a boiling-water canner for 5, 10, or 15 minutes depending on your altitude, according to the table that follows.

Full-Sugar Jam or Jelly Recommended process time in a boiling-water canner				
		Process time at altitudes of		
Style of pack	**Jar size**	**0–1,000 ft**	**1,001–6,000 ft**	**Above 6,000 ft**
Hot	Half-pints or Pints	5 min	10	15

Low-sugar fruit spreads must be processed longer or stored in the refrigerator, as detailed in the following section.

MAKING LOW-SUGAR FRUIT SPREADS

You can make a variety of fruit spreads that are tasty yet lower in sugar and calories than regular jams and jellies. The sweetening can come from the fruit itself; from apple or grape juice; from liquid low-calorie sweetener; or from a combination of these. The gelling can come from commercially prepared modified pectin or gelatin.

One form of modified pectin gels with less sugar than regular pectin. Another, which requires no added sugar at all, gels with calcium, which may be included in the package. To use modified pectin, follow the recipes and processing instructions that come with the package.

Gelatin can be used in place of pectin as a thickening agent, but in this case, the jars should not be processed. Instead, store them in the refrigerator, and use them up within 4 weeks.

PEACH-PINEAPPLE SPREAD

4 to 6 pounds firm ripe peaches
2 cups drained unsweetened crushed pineapple
¼ cup bottled lemon juice
Sugar (optional)

YIELD: 5 to 6 half-pints

PROCEDURE: Thoroughly wash and drain the peaches. Blanch them in boiling water for 30 to 60 seconds to loosen their skins. Then dip the peaches in cold water, and slip off the skins. Halve the peaches, and pit them. Cut the flesh into pieces. Grind the pieces in a food grinder, using a medium or coarse blade, or crush them with a fork (do not use a blender). Put the ground or crushed fruit into a large saucepan.

Heat the fruit slowly, stirring constantly, until it is tender. Put the cooked fruit into a jelly bag or into a colander lined with 4 layers of cheesecloth. Allow the juice to drip for about 15 minutes. Save the juice for jelly or another use. Measure out 4 cups of the drained fruit pulp. Combine this pulp with the pineapple and lemon juice in a pot. Add up to 2 cups sugar, as you prefer, and mix well. Bring the mixture to a boil, and boil it gently for 10 to 15 minutes, stirring often to prevent sticking. Remove the pot from the heat. Quickly fill hot half-pint or pint jars with the mixture, leaving ¼ inch headspace. Wipe the rims of the jars with a clean, dampened paper towel; apply the preheated lids and screw bands; and process the jars as indicated in the table that follows.

VARIATIONS: You can use nectarines, apricots, or plums in place of all or some of the peaches. You can also substitute noncaloric or low-calorie sweeteners for sugar. But keep in mind that if you use aspartame, a low-calorie sweetener, its sweetening power may be lost in 3 to 4 weeks.

Peach-Pineapple Spread					
Recommended process time in a boiling-water canner					
		Process time at altitudes of			
Style of pack	Jar size	0–1,000 ft	1,001–3,000 ft	3,001–6,000	Above 6,000 ft
Hot	Half-pints	15 min	20	20	25
	Pints	20	25	30	35

REFRIGERATED APPLE SPREAD
(MADE WITH GELATIN)

2 tbsp unflavored gelatin powder
1 quart unsweetened apple juice
2 tbsp bottled lemon juice
2 tbsp liquid low-calorie sweetener
Food coloring (optional)
YIELD: 4 half-pints

PROCEDURE: In a saucepan, soften the gelatin in the apple and lemon juices. Then dissolve the gelatin by bringing the mixture to a full rolling boil and boiling it for 2 minutes. Remove the pan from the heat. Stir in the sweetener and, if you like, food coloring. Fill half-pint jars with the spread, leaving ¼ inch headspace. Wipe the rims with a clean, dampened paper towel. Cap the jars, but do not process or freeze them. Instead, refrigerate them, and use them up within 4 weeks.

VARIATION: For spiced apple jelly, add 2 one-inch-long cinnamon sticks and 4 whole cloves to the mixture before boiling it. Remove the spices before adding the sweetener and food coloring.

REFRIGERATED GRAPE SPREAD
(MADE WITH GELATIN)

2 tbsp unflavored gelatin powder
3 cups (24 oz) unsweetened grape juice
2 tbsp bottled lemon juice
2 tbsp liquid low-calorie sweetener

YIELD: 3 half-pints

PROCEDURE: In a saucepan, soften the gelatin in the grape and lemon juices. Dissolve the gelatin by bringing the mixture to a full rolling boil and boiling it for 1 minute. Remove the pan from the heat, and stir in the sweetener. Quickly fill hot jars with the mixture, leaving ¼ inch headspace. Wipe the rims of the jars with a clean, dampened paper towel, and cap the jars, but do not process or freeze them. Instead, refrigerate them, and use them up within 4 weeks.

REMAKING SOFT JELLIES

If your jelly doesn't gel, you can remake it. Work with no more than 6 cups of jelly at a time. Use any of the following methods.

REMAKING JELLY WITH POWDERED PECTIN

For 4 cups of jelly, mix ¼ cup of sugar, ½ cup of water, 2 tablespoons of bottled lemon juice, and 4 teaspoons of powdered pectin in a pot. Bring the mixture to a boil while stirring. Add the jelly, and bring the mixture to a rolling boil over high heat, stirring constantly. Boil the mixture hard for 30 seconds. Remove the pot from the heat, quickly skim off any foam, and fill sterilized pint or half-pint jars (see page 53) with the jelly, leaving ¼ inch headspace. Wipe the rims of the jars with a clean, dampened paper towel. Apply new, preheated lids; screw on the bands; and process the jars as indicated in the table on page 147.

REMAKING JELLY WITH LIQUID PECTIN

For 4 cups of jelly, measure out ¾ cup of sugar, 2 tablespoons of bottled lemon juice, and 2 tablespoons of liquid pectin. Put the jelly into a pot. While stirring over high heat, bring the jelly to a boil. Remove the pot from the heat, and quickly add the sugar, lemon juice, and pectin. Bring the mixture to a full rolling boil, stirring constantly, and boil it hard for 1 minute. Quickly skim off any foam, and fill sterilized pint or half-pint jars (see page 53) with the jelly, leaving ¼ inch headspace. Wipe the rims of the jars with a clean, dampened paper towel. Apply new, preheated lids; screw on the bands; and process the jars as indicated in the table on page 147.

REMAKING JELLY WITHOUT ADDED PECTIN

Jelly may fail to set if it is too low in acid. To remedy this problem, combine 4 cups of the jelly with 2 tablespoons of bottled lemon juice in a pot. Heat the mixture to boiling, boil it for 3 to 4 minutes, then test it to determine if it has gelled. When it has, remove the pot from the heat, quickly skim off any foam, and fill sterilized pint or half-pint jars (see page 53) with the jelly, leaving ¼ inch headspace. Wipe the rims of the jars with a clean, dampened paper towel. Apply new, preheated lids; screw on the bands; and process the jars as indicated in the table on page 147.

TOMATOES & TOMATO PRODUCTS

Keep the following in mind when you're preparing to can tomatoes or tomato-based products:

QUALITY: Select only disease-free, firm tomatoes for canning. For best flavor, the tomatoes should be ripened on the vine—if they're ripened at all. Green tomatoes are actually more acidic than ripe ones and so can be canned safely with any of the methods in this chapter. **Do not can tomatoes from dead or frost-killed vines.**

ACIDIFICATION: To ensure a safe level of acidity in whole, crushed, or juiced tomatoes, add 2 tablespoons of bottled lemon juice or ½ teaspoon of citric acid per quart (1 tablespoon of bottled lemon juice or ¼ teaspoon of citric acid per pint). Put the lemon juice or citric acid directly into the jars before you fill them with tomatoes. You may add sugar to offset the extra acidity.

If you'd prefer to acidify your tomatoes with vinegar, you'll need to use 4 tablespoons of vinegar with 5 percent acidity for each quart of tomatoes (2 tablespoons per pint). The vinegar will affect the flavor more than the lemon juice or citric acid would.

Certain recipes in this chapter include instructions for both boiling-water and pressure canners. Although all the steps prior to processing—including acidification—are the same, using a pressure canner for these will result in better, more nutritious products.

TOMATO JUICE

Heating tomatoes fast keeps the juice from separating.

QUANTITY: A quart jar holds the juice of about 3¼ pounds of tomatoes. So you'll need about 23 pounds of tomatoes to fill 7 quart jars or about 14 pounds to fill 9 pint jars. A bushel of tomatoes weighs 53 pounds and yields 15 to 18 quarts of juice.

PROCEDURE: Wash and stem the tomatoes, and trim off any bruised or discolored areas. To keep the juice from separating, quickly quarter about 1 pound of the tomatoes, and crush them in a pot with a wooden mallet or spoon as you heat them to boiling over high heat. Continue to add freshly cut tomato quarters to the boiling mixture, crushing them as you go. Make sure the mixture boils constantly and vigorously while you add the remaining tomatoes. When you've added all of the tomatoes, simmer them for 5 minutes. (If you aren't concerned about juice separation, you can slice or quarter all of the tomatoes before crushing and simmering them.) Press the hot, crushed tomatoes through a sieve or food mill to remove the skins and seeds. Add bottled lemon juice or citric acid to hot jars, as specified on page 154. If you like, you can add 1 teaspoon of salt per quart. Heat the tomato juice to boiling again, then pour it into the jars, leaving ½ inch headspace. Wipe the rims of the jars with a clean, dampened paper towel; apply the preheated lids and screw bands; and process the jars in a boiling-water or pressure canner as indicated in the tables that follow.

Tomato Juice					
Recommended process time in a boiling-water canner					
Style of pack	Jar size	Process time at altitudes of			
		0–1,000 ft	1,001–3,000 ft	3,001–6,000 ft	Above 6,000 ft
Hot	Pints	35 min	40	45	50
	Quarts	40	45	50	55

Tomato Juice Recommended process time in a dial-gauge pressure canner						
Style of pack	**Jar size**	**Process time**	**Canner pressure (PSI) at altitudes of**			
			0–2,000 ft	**2,001–4,000 ft**	**4,001–6,000 ft**	**6,001–8,000 ft**
Hot	Pints or Quarts	20 min	6 lb	7 lb	8 lb	9 lb
		15	11	12	13	14

Tomato Juice Recommended process time in a weighted-gauge pressure canner				
Style of pack	**Jar size**	**Process time**	**Canner pressure (PSI) at altitudes of**	
			0–1,000 ft	**Above 1,000 ft**
Hot	Pints or Quarts	20 min	5 lb	10 lb
		15	10	15
		10	15	Not recommended

TOMATO AND VEGETABLE JUICE BLEND

QUANTITY: You'll need about 22 pounds of tomatoes to fill 7 quart jars. Add no more than 3 cups of other vegetables for each 22 pounds of tomatoes.

PROCEDURE: Crush and simmer the tomatoes as in the preceding recipe. Add no more than 3 cups of finely chopped vegetables—celery, onions, carrots, peppers, or any combination of these—for each 22 pounds of tomatoes. Simmer the mixture for 20 minutes. Press the hot mixture through a sieve or food mill to remove skins and seeds. Put bottled lemon juice or citric acid in hot jars, as specified on page 154. If you like, add 1 teaspoon of salt per quart. Heat the juice to boiling, then immediately pour it into the jars, leaving ½ inch headspace. Wipe the rims of the jars with a clean, dampened paper towel; apply the preheated lids and screw bands; and process the jars in a boiling-water or pressure canner as indicated in the tables that follow.

Tomato and Vegetable Juice Blend
Recommended process time in a boiling-water canner

Style of pack	Jar size	Process time at altitudes of			
		0–1,000 ft	1,001–3,000 ft	3,001–6,000 ft	Above 6,000 ft
Hot	Pints	35 min	40	45	50
	Quarts	40	45	50	55

Tomato and Vegetable Juice Blend
Recommended process time in a dial-gauge pressure canner

Style of pack	Jar size	Process time	Canner pressure (PSI) at altitudes of			
			0–2,000 ft	2,001–4,000 ft	4,001–6,000 ft	6,001–8,000 ft
Hot	Pints or Quarts	20 min	6 lb	7 lb	8 lb	9 lb
		15	11	12	13	14

Tomato and Vegetable Juice Blend
Recommended process time in a weighted-gauge pressure canner

Style of pack	Jar size	Process time	Canner pressure (PSI) at altitudes of	
			0–1,000 ft	Above 1,000 ft
Hot	Pints or Quarts	20 min	5 lb	10 lb
		15	10	15
		10	15	Not recommended

STANDARD TOMATO SAUCE

QUANTITY: A quart jar holds about 5 pounds of tomatoes as thin sauce or about 6½ pounds as thick sauce. For thin sauce, therefore, you'll need about 35 pounds of tomatoes to fill 7 quart jars or about 21 pounds to fill 9 pint jars. For thick sauce, you'll need about 46 pounds of tomatoes to fill 7 quart jars or about 28 pounds to fill 9 pint jars. A bushel of tomatoes weighs 53 pounds and yields 10 to 12 quarts of thin sauce or 7 to 9 quarts of thick sauce.

PROCEDURE: Make tomato juice as described on pages 157–158. In a wide pan, simmer the juice to the thickness you prefer. For a thin sauce, reduce the juice by about ⅓. For a thick sauce, reduce it by about ½. Put bottled lemon juice or citric acid into hot jars as specified on page 154. If you like, add 1 teaspoon of salt per quart. Fill the jars with the hot sauce, leaving ¼ inch headspace. Remove the air bubbles, and adjust the headspace if needed. Wipe the rims of the jars with a clean, dampened paper towel; apply the preheated lids and screw bands; and process the jars as indicated in the tables that follow.

Standard Tomato Sauce					
Recommended process time in a boiling-water canner					
Style of pack	Jar size	Process time at altitudes of			
		0–1,000 ft	1,001–3,000 ft	3,001–6,000 ft	Above 6,000 ft
Hot	Pints	35 min	40	45	50
	Quarts	40	45	50	55

Standard Tomato Sauce						
Recommended process time in a dial-gauge pressure canner						
Style of pack	Jar size	Process time	Canner pressure (PSI) at altitudes of			
			0–2,000 ft	2,001–4,000 ft	4,001–6,000 ft	6,001–8,000 ft
Hot	Pints or Quarts	20 min	6 lb	7 lb	8 lb	9 lb
		15	11	12	13	14

			Canner pressure (PSI) at altitudes of	
Standard Tomato Sauce Recommended process time in a weighted-gauge pressure canner				
Style of pack	**Jar size**	**Process time**	**0–1,000 ft**	**Above 1,000 ft**
Hot	Pints or Quarts	20 min	5 lb	10 lb
		15	10	15
		10	15	Not recommended

TOMATOES—WHOLE OR HALVED
(PACKED IN WATER)

QUANTITY: A quart jar holds about 3 pounds of whole or halved tomatoes. You'll therefore need about 21 pounds of tomatoes to fill 7 quart jars or 13 pounds to fill 9 pint jars. A bushel weighs 53 pounds and yields 15 to 21 quarts of whole or halved tomatoes.

PROCEDURE: Wash the tomatoes. Dip them in boiling water for 30 to 60 seconds or until their skins split. Then dip the tomatoes in cold water, and slip off their skins. Core the tomatoes, and halve them if they're large. Put bottled lemon juice or citric acid into hot jars, as specified on page 154. If you like, add 1 teaspoon of salt per quart.

If you're hot-packing the tomatoes, put them into a pot, add enough water to cover them, and boil them gently for 5 minutes. Fill the jars with the hot tomatoes, and add enough hot cooking liquid to cover the tomatoes, leaving ½ inch headspace.

If you're raw-packing the tomatoes, bring some water to a boil. Fill the jars with the raw tomatoes, and add enough boiling water to cover the tomatoes, leaving ½ inch headspace.

Remove the air bubbles, and adjust the headspace if needed. Wipe the rims of the jars with a clean, dampened paper towel; apply the preheated lids and screw bands; and process the jars as indicated in the tables that follow.

Water-Packed Whole Tomatoes
Recommended process time in a boiling-water canner

Style of pack	Jar size	Process time at altitudes of			
		0–1,000 ft	1,001–3,000 ft	3,001–6,000 ft	Above 6,000 ft
Hot or Raw	Pints	40 min	45	50	55
	Quarts	45	50	55	60

Water-Packed Whole Tomatoes
Recommended process time in a dial-gauge pressure canner

Style of pack	Jar size	Process time	Canner pressure (PSI) at altitudes of			
			0–2,000 ft	2,001–4,000 ft	4,001–6,000 ft	6,001–8,000 ft
Hot or Raw	Pints or Quarts	15 min	6 lb	7 lb	8 lb	9 lb
		10	11	12	13	14

Water-Packed Whole Tomatoes
Recommended process time in a weighted-gauge pressure canner

Style of pack	Jar size	Process time	Canner pressure (PSI) at altitudes of	
			0–1,000 ft	Above 1,000 ft
Hot or Raw	Pints or Quarts	15 min	5 lb	10 lb
		10	10	15
		1	15	Not recommended

TOMATOES—WHOLE OR HALVED
(PACKED IN TOMATO JUICE)

QUANTITY: The quantities are the same as in the previous recipe, but you'll need to make some tomatoes into juice.

PROCEDURE: Wash the tomatoes. Dip them in boiling water for 30 to 60 seconds or until their skins split. Then dip the tomatoes in cold water, and slip off their skins. Core the tomatoes, and halve them if they're large. Put bottled lemon juice or citric acid into hot jars, as specified on page 154. If you like, add 1 teaspoon of salt per quart.

If you're hot-packing the tomatoes, put them into a pot, cover them with juice, and boil them gently for 5 minutes. Fill the jars with the hot tomatoes, and cover them with the hot juice, leaving ½ inch headspace.

If you're raw-packing the tomatoes, heat the tomato juice in a saucepan. Fill the jars with the raw tomatoes, and cover them with the hot juice, leaving ½ inch headspace.

Remove the air bubbles, and adjust the headspace if needed. Wipe the rims of the jars with a clean, dampened paper towel; apply the preheated lids and screw bands; and process the jars as indicated in the tables that follow.

Tomato-Juice-Packed Whole Tomatoes Recommended process time in a boiling-water canner					
Style of pack	Jar size	Process time at altitudes of			
		0–1,000 ft	1,001–3,000 ft	3,001–6,000 ft	Above 6,000 ft
Hot or Raw	Pints or Quarts	85 min	90	95	100

Tomato-Juice-Packed Whole Tomatoes Recommended process time in a dial-gauge pressure canner						
Style of pack	Jar size	Process time	Canner pressure (PSI) at altitudes of			
			0–2,000 ft	2,001–4,000 ft	4,001–6,000 ft	6,001–8,000 ft
Hot or Raw	Pints or Quarts	40 min	6 lb	7 lb	8 lb	9 lb
		25	11	12	13	14

Tomato-Juice-Packed Whole Tomatoes Recommended process time in a weighted-gauge pressure canner				
Style of pack	Jar size	Process time	Canner pressure (PSI) at altitudes of	
			0–1,000 ft	Above 1,000 ft
Hot or	Pints or	40 min	5 lb	10 lb

Tomato-Juice-Packed Whole Tomatoes				
Recommended process time in a weighted-gauge pressure canner				
			Canner pressure (PSI) at altitudes of	
Raw	Quarts	25	10	15
		15	15	Not recommended

TOMATOES–WHOLE OR HALVED

(PACKED RAW WITHOUT ADDED LIQUID)

QUANTITY: See "Tomatoes–Whole or Halved (packed in water)," on page 160.

PROCEDURE: Wash the tomatoes. Dip them in boiling water for 30 to 60 seconds or until their skins split. Then dip the tomatoes in cold water, and slip off their skins. Core the tomatoes, and halve them if they're large. Put bottled lemon juice or citric acid into hot jars, as specified on page 154. If you like, add 1 teaspoon of salt per quart. Fill the jars with the raw tomatoes, pressing them down so the spaces between them fill with their juice and leaving ½ inch headspace. Remove the air bubbles, and adjust the headspace if needed. Wipe the rims of the jars with a clean, dampened paper towel; apply the preheated lids and screw bands; and process the jars as indicated in the tables that follow.

Raw Whole Tomatoes without Added Liquid					
Recommended process time in a boiling-water canner					
Style of pack	Jar size	Process time at altitudes of			
		0–1,000 ft	1,001–3,000 ft	3,001–6,000 ft	Above 6,000 ft
Raw	Pints or Quarts	85 min	90	95	100

Raw Whole Tomatoes without Added Liquid
Recommended process time in a dial-gauge pressure canner

Style of pack	Jar size	Process time	Canner pressure (PSI) at altitudes of			
			0–2,000 ft	2,001–4,000 ft	4,001–6,000 ft	6,001–8,000 ft
Raw	Pints or Quarts	40 min	6 lb	7 lb	8 lb	9 lb
		25	11	12	13	14

Raw Whole Tomatoes without Added Liquid
Recommended process time in a weighted-gauge pressure canner

Style of pack	Jar size	Process time	Canner pressure (PSI) at altitudes of	
			0–1,000 ft	Above 1,000 ft
Raw	Pints or Quarts	40 min	5 lb	10 lb
		25	10	15
		15	15	Not recommended

SPAGHETTI SAUCE WITHOUT MEAT

The proportion of tomatoes relative to other vegetables is essential to the acid level—and safe canning—of this sauce. **Do not increase the proportion of onions, peppers, or mushrooms.**

30 lbs tomatoes
¼ cup vegetable oil
1 cup chopped onions
5 garlic cloves, minced
1 cup chopped celery or green peppers
1 lb fresh mushrooms, sliced (optional)
2 tbsp dried oregano
4 tbsp minced parsley
2 tsp ground black pepper
4½ tsp salt
¼ cup packed brown sugar

YIELD: About 9 pints

PROCEDURE: Wash the tomatoes. Dip them in boiling water for 30 to 60 seconds or until their skins split. Dip the tomatoes in cold water, and slip off the skins. Core and quarter the tomatoes. In a large pot, boil them, uncovered, for 20 minutes. Then put the tomatoes through a food mill or sieve to purée them. Heat the vegetable oil in a pan. Add the onions, garlic, celery or peppers, and, if you like, mushrooms. Sauté the vegetables until they are tender. Combine them in a pot with the puréed tomatoes; add the oregano, parsley, black pepper, salt, and brown sugar; and bring the mixture to a boil. Stir frequently as you simmer it, uncovered, until it is reduced by nearly half. Fill hot pint or quart jars with the sauce, leaving 1 inch headspace. Remove the air bubbles, and adjust the headspace if needed. Wipe the rims of the jars with a clean, dampened paper towel; apply the preheated lids and screw bands; and process the jars in a pressure canner as indicated in the tables that follow.

Spaghetti Sauce without Meat
Recommended process time in a dial-gauge pressure canner

Style of pack	Jar size	Process time	Canner pressure (PSI) at altitudes of			
			0–2,000 ft	2,001–4,000 ft	4,001–6,000 ft	6,001–8,000 ft
Hot	Pints	20 min	11 lb	12 lb	13 lb	14 lb
	Quarts	25	11	12	13	14

Spaghetti Sauce without Meat
Recommended process time in a weighted-gauge pressure canner

Style of pack	Jar size	Process time	Canner pressure (PSI) at altitudes of	
			0–1,000 ft	Above 1,000 ft
Hot	Pints	20 min	10 lb	15 lb
	Quarts	25	10	15

SPAGHETTI SAUCE WITH MEAT

30 lbs tomatoes

2½ lbs ground beef or sausage

5 garlic cloves, minced

1 cup chopped onions

1 cup chopped celery or green peppers

1 lb fresh mushrooms, sliced (optional)

2 tbsp dried oregano

4 tbsp minced parsley

2 tsp ground black pepper

4½ tsp salt

¼ cup brown sugar

YIELD: About 9 pints

PROCEDURE: Peel, cook, and purée the tomatoes as in the preceding recipe. In a large pan, sauté the ground beef or sausage until it is brown. Add the garlic, onion, celery or green pepper, and, if you like, mushrooms. Cook until the vegetables are tender. Combine the vegetables and meat with the tomato purée in a large pot. Add the oregano, parsley, black pepper, salt, and sugar, and bring the mixture to a boil. Stir frequently as you simmer the mixture, uncovered, until it is reduced by half. Fill hot pint or quart jars with the sauce, leaving 1 inch headspace. Remove the air bubbles, and adjust the headspace if needed. Wipe the rims of the jars with a clean, dampened paper towel; apply the preheated lids and screw bands; and process the jars in a pressure canner as indicated in the tables that follow.

Spaghetti Sauce with Meat						
Recommended process time in a dial-gauge pressure canner						
Style of pack	Jar size	Process time	Canner pressure (PSI) at altitudes of			
			0–2,000 ft	2,001–4,000 ft	4,001–6,000 ft	6,001–8,000 ft
Hot	Pints	60 min	11 lb	12 lb	13 lb	14 lb
	Quarts	70	11	12	13	14

			Canner pressure (PSI) at altitudes of	
Style of pack	Jar size	Process time	0–1,000 ft	Above 1,000 ft
Hot	Pints	60 min	10 lb	15 lb
	Quarts	70	10	15

Spaghetti Sauce with Meat
Recommended process time in a weighted-gauge pressure canner

EASY HOT SAUCE

Serrano peppers are very hot. Wear plastic or rubber gloves when handling them, and avoid touching your eyes or face.

2 tbsp whole mixed pickling spices
8 cups (64 ounces) canned diced tomatoes, undrained
1½ cups seeded, chopped serrano peppers
4 cups distilled white vinegar (5% acidity)
2 tsp canning and pickling salt

YIELD: About 4 half-pints

PROCEDURE: Tie the spices in a spice bag or 2 layers of cheesecloth, and put the bundle into a large pot with all of the other ingredients. Bring the mixture to a boil, stirring occasionally. Reduce the heat, and simmer the mixture for 20 minutes, until the tomatoes are soft. Remove the spice bag, and press the mixture through a food mill. Return the resulting sauce to the pot, heat the sauce to boiling, and boil it for 15 minutes. Fill hot half-pint jars with the sauce, leaving ¼ inch headspace. Remove the air bubbles, and adjust the headspace if needed. Wipe the rims of the jars with a clean, dampened paper towel; apply the preheated lids and screw bands; and process the jars in a boiling-water canner as indicated in the table on the next page.

Easy Hot Sauce				
Recommended process time in a boiling-water canner				
		Process time at altitudes of		
Style of pack	Jar size	0–1,000 ft	1,001–6,000 ft	Above 6,000 ft
Hot	Half-pints	10 min	15	20

TOMATO KETCHUP

24 lbs ripe tomatoes

3 cups chopped onions

¾ tsp ground dried hot pepper

3 cups cider vinegar (5% acidity)

4 tsp whole cloves

3 one-inch-long cinnamon sticks, crushed

1½ tsp whole allspice

3 tbsp celery seeds

1½ cups sugar

¼ cup canning and pickling salt

YIELD: 6 to 7 pints

PROCEDURE: Wash the tomatoes. Dip them in boiling water for 30 to 60 seconds or until their skins split. Dip the tomatoes in cold water, and slip off skins. Core and quarter the tomatoes. Put them into a large pot with the onions and ground dried hot pepper. Bring the mixture to a boil, and simmer it, uncovered, for 20 minutes. Cover the pot, turn off the heat, and let the mixture stand for 20 minutes. Put the vinegar into a saucepan. Tie the cloves, cinnamon, allspice, and celery seeds in a spice bag or 2 layers of cheesecloth, and add the bundle to the vinegar. Bring the vinegar to a boil. Remove the spice bag, and pour the vinegar into the pot with the tomatoes. Boil the mixture about 30 minutes. Put the boiled mixture through a food mill or sieve to purée it. Return it to the pot. Add the sugar and salt, and boil gently, stirring frequently, until the volume is reduced by half and the ketchup rounds on a spoon with no separation of liquid from solids. Fill hot pint jars with the ketchup, leaving ⅛ inch headspace.

Remove the air bubbles, and adjust the headspace if needed. Wipe the rims of the jars with a clean, dampened paper towel; apply the preheated lids and screw bands; and process the jars in a boiling-water canner as indicated in the table that follows.

Tomato Ketchup Recommended process time in a boiling-water canner				
		Process time at altitudes of		
Style of pack	Jar size	0–1,000 ft	1,001–6,000 ft	Above 6,000 ft
Hot	Pints	15 min	20	25

SALSAS

Like most salsas, those in this chapter are mixtures of low-acid foods, such as onions and peppers, and acid foods, such as tomatoes. When you're canning salsa, therefore, it's important to measure the ingredients carefully and follow the recipe exactly.

SELECTING AND PREPARING SALSA INGREDIENTS

ACIDS

Acid ingredients are added to canned salsa to help preserve it. Without these ingredients, the canned salsa may not be safe to eat. To ensure an adequate acidity level for boiling-water processing, the recipes here call for either commercially bottled lemon or lime juice or vinegar with 5% acidity. When preparing these recipes, **do not** replace bottled lemon or lime juice with fresh-squeezed, because the acidity of fresh juice varies. **Do not** use vinegar of unknown acidity or substitute vinegar for lemon or lime juice. (You can, however, substitute bottled lemon or lime juice for vinegar.) And **do not** reduce the amount of vinegar or lemon or lime juice called for. If the salsa is too tart for your taste, try adding sugar to balance the acid.

TOMATOES

The type of tomatoes you use will affect the consistency of your salsa. Paste tomatoes, such as Roma, are meatier and less juicy than slicing tomatoes and so will produce thicker salsa. Don't attempt to thicken your salsa by squeezing the tomatoes and discarding their juice. This would lessen the acidity of the salsa, potentially jeopardizing safety.

Do not use overripe or spoiling tomatoes for canning. Use only high-quality, disease-free, firm tomatoes, preferably vine-ripened, or your salsa will be thin and may even spoil. You can use green tomatoes or tomatillos in place of ripe tomatoes in these recipes, but if you do, the salsa will taste quite different.

PEPPERS

Peppers range from mild to scorching. Use only high-quality, unblemished peppers that are free of decay. You can use canned peppers in place of fresh, if you like. For stronger or milder salsa, you can substitute one type of pepper for another. But don't increase the total weight or volume of peppers or substitute the same number of large peppers for small ones (for example, don't use 6 bell or long green peppers in place of 6 jalapeños or serranos); either of these changes would lessen the acidity of your finished salsa and could possibly make it unsafe.

When a recipe calls for "long green peppers," choose a variety such as Anaheim, poblano, or Hungarian wax. When a recipe calls for jalapeño, you can substitute another small, hot variety such as cayenne, habanero, serrano, or tabasco.

If the juice of hot peppers comes in contact with the eyes, it can cause an intense burning sensation. **Wear plastic or rubber gloves when handling hot peppers, and avoid touching your eyes or face.**

If you're going to finely chop peppers for salsa, you probably don't need to peel them first. Many recipes say to peel long green peppers, however, because their skins can be tough after canning. To peel peppers, wash and dry them, then slit each pepper along the side; this will allow steam to escape when you blister the skins. Put the peppers in a hot oven (400°F) or under a broiler for 6 to 8 minutes or over a gas or electric burner covered with heavy wire mesh for several minutes. Place the blistered peppers in a pan, cover them with a damp cloth, and let them cool for several minutes, after which the skins should peel off easily.

SALT, SPICES, AND HERBS

You can add more or less salt, spices (black pepper, cumin), and dried oregano than the recipes call for. When a recipe calls for fresh cilantro, however, it's best to add more just before serving rather than before canning.

ONIONS

Red, yellow, and white onions can be used interchangeably. But don't increase the total volume or weight of onions in any recipe.

CANNING SALSA

Follow recipe directions carefully. Use peppers, onions, tomatoes, and vinegar or lemon or lime juice in the amounts specified; altering proportions could make the salsa unsafe. The only changes you can safely make in these recipes are substituting bottled lemon or lime juice for vinegar (but not the reverse); changing the amounts of salt, spices, and dried herbs; and adding sugar.

Process your salsa in a boiling-water canner as indicated in the table that follows.

Tomato Salsa Recommended process time in a boiling-water canner				
		Process time at altitudes of		
Style of pack	Jar size	0–1,000 ft	1,001–6,000 ft	Above 6,000 ft
Hot	Pints	15 min	20	25

If you've made salsa without following a recipe tested for safety, don't can the salsa. Freeze it or store it in the refrigerator instead.

CHILE SALSA (HOT TOMATO-PEPPER SAUCE)

2 lbs long green peppers, such as Anaheim
5 lbs tomatoes
1 lb onions
1 cup vinegar (5% acidity)
3 tsp canning and pickling salt
½ tsp ground black pepper

YIELD: About 6 to 8 pints

PROCEDURE: Wearing plastic or rubber gloves, wash, slit, blister, and peel the peppers as described on page 171. Seed and chop the peeled peppers. Wash the tomatoes, and dip them In boiling water for 30 to 60 seconds or until the skins split. Dip the tomatoes in cold water, slip off the skins, and core and coarsely chop the tomatoes. In a pot, combine the chopped tomatoes and peppers with the onions, vinegar, salt, and black pepper. Heat the mixture to boiling, reduce the heat, and simmer for 10 minutes. Fill hot pint jars with the salsa, leaving ½ inch headspace. Remove the air bubbles, and adjust the headspace if needed. Wipe the rims of the jars with a clean, dampened paper towel; apply the preheated lids and screw bands; and process the jars in a boiling-water canner as indicated in the table on page 172.

TOMATO SALSA USING PASTE TOMATOES

This recipe works best with paste tomatoes, such as Roma; slicing tomatoes require a much longer cooking time to thicken adequately. Prepare the tomatoes as directed in the previous recipe. **When handling hot peppers, wear plastic or rubber gloves, and avoid touching your eyes or face.** Peel the long green peppers or just wash them before seeding and chopping them.

7 quarts peeled, cored, and chopped tomatoes
4 cups seeded and chopped long green peppers, such as Anaheim
½ cup seeded and finely chopped jalapeño peppers
5 cups chopped onions
6 garlic cloves, finely chopped
2 cups bottled lemon or lime juice
2 tbsp canning and pickling salt
1 tbsp ground black pepper
2 tbsp ground cumin (optional)
3 tbsp dried oregano leaves (optional)
2 tbsp fresh cilantro (optional)

YIELD: About 16 to 18 pints

PROCEDURE: Combine the tomatoes, Anaheim and jalapeño peppers, onions, garlic, lemon or lime juice, salt, and black pepper in a large pot. Bring the mixture to a boil, stirring frequently. Reduce the heat, and simmer for 10 minutes. Add the cumin, oregano, and cilantro, and simmer for 20 minutes more, stirring occasionally. Fill hot pint jars with the hot salsa, leaving ½ inch headspace. Remove the air bubbles, and adjust the headspace if needed. Wipe the rims of the jars with a clean, dampened paper towel; apply the preheated lids and screw bands; and process the jars in a boiling-water canner as indicated in the table on page 172.

TOMATO SALSA USING SLICING TOMATOES

Prepare the tomatoes as directed for Chili Salsa (page 173). **When handling hot peppers, wear plastic or rubber gloves, and avoid touching your eyes or face.** Peel the long green peppers as described on page 171, or just wash them before seeding and chopping them.

4 cups peeled, cored, and chopped slicing tomatoes
2 cups seeded and chopped long green peppers,
such as Anaheim
$1/2$ cup seeded and chopped jalapeño peppers
$3/4$ cup chopped onions
4 garlic cloves, finely chopped
2 cups vinegar (5% acidity)
$1 1/2$ tsp canning and pickling salt
1 tsp ground cumin (optional)
1 tbsp oregano leaves (optional)
1 tbsp fresh cilantro (optional)

YIELD: About 4 pints

PROCEDURE: Combine all ingredients in a large pot. Bring the mixture to a boil, stirring frequently. Reduce the heat, and simmer for 20 minutes, stirring occasionally. Fill hot pint jars with the hot salsa, leaving ½ inch headspace. Remove the air bubbles, and adjust the headspace if needed. Wipe the rims of the jars with a clean, dampened paper towel; apply the preheated lids and screw bands; and process the jars in a boiling-water canner as indicated in the table on page 172.

VEGETABLES & VEGETABLE PRODUCTS

ASPARAGUS— SPEARS OR PIECES

QUANTITY: A quart jar holds about 3½ pounds of asparagus spears or pieces. You'll therefore need about 24½ pounds of asparagus to fill 7 quart jars or about 16 pounds to fill 9 pint jars. A crate of asparagus weighs 31 pounds and yields 7 to 12 quarts.

QUALITY: Use tender, tight spear tips that are 4 to 6 inches long.

PROCEDURE: Wash the asparagus, break off the tough lower stems, and trim off any tough scales on the upper portions. Wash the asparagus again. If you like, cut it into 1-inch pieces. If you're hot-packing the asparagus, put it into a pan, cover it with boiling water, and boil it for 2 to 3 minutes. Loosely fill hot pint or quart jars with the boiled or raw asparagus, leaving 1 inch headspace. If you like, add ½ teaspoon of canning and pickling salt per pint to the jars. Then add freshly boiled water to just cover the asparagus, leaving 1 inch headspace. Remove the air bubbles, and adjust the headspace if needed. Wipe the rims of the jars with a clean, dampened paper towel; apply the preheated lids and the screw bands; and process the jars in a pressure canner according to the tables on page 178.

Asparagus						
Recommended process time in a dial-gauge pressure canner						
Style of pack	Jar size	Process time	Canner pressure (PSI) at altitudes of			
			0–2,000 ft	2,001–4,000 ft	4,001–6,000 ft	6,001–8,000 ft
Hot or Raw	Pints	30 min	11 lb	12 lb	13 lb	14 lb
	Quarts	40	11	12	13	14

Asparagus				
Recommended process time in a weighted-gauge pressure canner				
Style of pack	Jar size	Process time	Canner pressure (PSI) at altitudes of	
			0–1,000 ft	Above 1,000 ft
Hot or Raw	Pints	30 min	10 lb	15 lb
	Quarts	40	10	15

BEANS, SNAP OR ITALIAN—PIECES

In this recipe, you can use string beans, yellow wax beans, or flat beans such as Romano.

QUANTITY: A quart jar holds about 2 pounds of green beans. You'll therefore need about 14 pounds of beans to fill 7 quart jars or about 9 pounds to fill 9 pint jars. A bushel of green beans weighs 30 pounds and yields 12 to 20 quarts.

QUALITY: Select filled but tender, crisp pods. Remove and discard any beans that have rust spots or other signs of disease.

PROCEDURE: Wash the beans, and trim off their ends. If you prefer, break or cut the beans into 1-inch-long pieces. To hot-pack the beans, put them into a pot, cover them with boiling water, boil them 5 minutes, and pack them loosely into hot pint or quart jars. To raw-pack the beans, pack them tightly into hot jars. Whether you're hot- or raw-packing, leave 1 inch headspace. If you like, add ½ teaspoon of canning and pickling salt per pint to the jars.

Then add boiling water to just cover the beans, keeping the 1 inch headspace. Remove the air bubbles, and adjust the headspace if needed. Wipe the rims of the jars with a clean, dampened paper towel; apply the preheated lids and the screw bands; and process the jars in a pressure canner according to the tables that follow.

Snap or Italian Beans
Recommended process time in a dial-gauge pressure canner

Style of pack	Jar size	Process time	Canner pressure (PSI) at altitudes of			
			0–2,000 ft	2,001–4,000 ft	4,001–6,000 ft	6,001–8,000 ft
Hot or Raw	Pints	20 min	11 lb	12 lb	13 lb	14 lb
	Quarts	25	11	12	13	14

Snap or Italian Beans
Recommended process time in a weighted-gauge pressure canner

Style of pack	Jar size	Process time	Canner pressure (PSI) at altitudes of	
			0–1,000 ft	Above 1,000 ft
Hot or Raw	Pints	20 min	10 lb	15 lb
	Quarts	25	10	15

BEANS OR PEAS, DRIED—SHELLED

Use shelled dried beans or peas of any variety in this recipe.

QUANTITY: A quart jar holds about ¾ pound of cooked shelled beans or peas. You'll therefore need about 5 pounds of dried beans or peas to fill 7 quart jars or about 3¼ pounds to fill 9 pint jars.

QUALITY: Select mature, dried bean or pea seeds. Sort out and discard any that are discolored.

PROCEDURE: Rinse the sorted beans or peas. Put them into a large pot, and cover them with water. Let them soak for 12 to 18 hours in a cool place, then drain them. (To hydrate beans faster, cover them with boiling water, boil them for 2 minutes, and remove the pot from the heat. Let the beans soak for 1 hour, then drain them.) Cover the soaked beans with fresh water, and boil them for 30 minutes. If you like, add ½ teaspoon of canning and pickling salt per pint to the hot jars. Fill the jars with the hot beans or peas and cooking liquid, leaving 1 inch headspace. Remove the air bubbles, and adjust the headspace if needed. Wipe the rims of the jars with a clean, dampened paper towel; apply the preheated lids and the screw bands; and process the jars in a pressure canner according to the tables that follow.

			Beans or Peas Recommended process time in a dial-gauge pressure canner			
Style of pack	Jar size	Process time	Canner pressure (PSI) at altitudes of			
			0–2,000 ft	2,001–4,000 ft	4,001–6,000 ft	6,001–8,000 ft
Hot	Pints	75 min	11 lb	12 lb	13 lb	14 lb
	Quarts	90	11	12	13	14

			Canner pressure (PSI) at altitudes of	
Beans or Peas Recommended process time in a weighted-gauge pressure canner				
Style of pack	Jar size	Process time	0–1,000 ft	Above 1,000 ft
Hot	Pints	75 min	10 lb	15 lb
	Quarts	90	10	15

BEETS—WHOLE, CUBED, OR SLICED

QUANTITY: A quart jar holds about 3 pounds of beets. You'll therefore need about 21 pounds of beets without tops to fill 7 quart jars or about 13½ pounds to fill 9 pint jars. A bushel of beets without tops weighs 52 pounds and yields 15 to 20 quarts.

QUALITY: Use beets no larger than 3 inches in diameter; bigger beets can be fibrous. If you're packing the beets whole, they should be no more than 2 inches in diameter.

PROCEDURE: Trim off the beet tops, leaving an inch of both stem and root to help reduce bleeding of color. Scrub beets well. Put them in a pot, cover them with boiling water, and boil them until their skins slip off easily, about 15 to 25 minutes, depending on size. Let the beets cool, and remove their skins. Trim off the stems and roots. Cut medium or large beets into ½-inch cubes or slices. Halve or quarter very large slices. Bring enough fresh water to a boil to cover the beets in the jars. If you like, add ½ teaspoon of canning and pickling salt per pint to the hot jars. Fill the jars with the hot beets and hot water, leaving 1 inch headspace. Remove the air bubbles, and adjust the headspace if needed. Wipe the rims of the jars with a clean, dampened paper towel; apply the preheated lids and the screw bands; and process the jars in a pressure canner according to the tables on the next page.

Beets						
Recommended process time for Beets in a dial-gauge pressure canner						
			Canner pressure (PSI) at altitudes of			
Style of pack	Jar size	Process time	0–2,000 ft	2,001–4,000 ft	4,001–6,000 ft	6,001–8,000 ft
Hot	Pints	30 min	11 lb	12 lb	13 lb	14 lb
	Quarts	35	11	12	13	14

Beets				
Recommended process time for Beets in a weighted-gauge pressure canner				
			Canner pressure (PSI) at altitudes of	
Style of pack	Jar size	Process time	0–1,000 ft	Above 1,000 ft
Hot	Pints	30 min	10 lb	15 lb
	Quarts	35	10	15

CARROTS—SLICED OR DICED

QUANTITY: A quart jar holds about 2½ pounds of carrots. You'll therefore need about 17½ pounds of carrots (without their green, parsleylike tops) to fill 7 quart jars or about 11 pounds to fill 9 pint jars. A bushel of carrots (without their tops) weighs 50 pounds and yields 17 to 25 quarts of canned carrots.

QUALITY: Select small carrots, preferably those that are 1 inch to 1¼ inches in diameter at their widest point. Larger carrots are often too fibrous.

PROCEDURE: Wash, peel, and then rewash the carrots. Slice or dice them, whichever you prefer. If you're hot-packing, put the carrots into a pot; cover them with boiling water; bring the water to a boil; and simmer the carrots for 5 minutes. Then pack the carrots into hot pint or quart jars, leaving 1 inch headspace. If you're raw-packing, pack the raw carrots loosely into hot jars, leaving 1 inch headspace, and bring to a boil enough water to cover them. If you like, add ½ teaspoon of canning and pickling salt per pint to the jars. Pour the hot cooking liquid or hot water over the carrots, maintaining the 1 inch headspace.

Remove the air bubbles, and adjust the headspace if needed. Wipe the rims of the jars with a clean, dampened paper towel; apply the preheated lids and the screw bands; and process the jars in a pressure canner according to the tables that follow.

Carrots						
Recommended process time in a dial-gauge pressure canner						
			Canner pressure (PSI) at altitudes of			
Style of pack	Jar size	Process time	0–2,000 ft	2,001–4,000 ft	4,001–6,000 ft	6,001–8,000 ft
Hot or Raw	Pints	25 min	11 lb	12 lb	13 lb	14 lb
	Quarts	30	11	12	13	14

Carrots				
Recommended process time in a weighted-gauge pressure canner				
			Canner pressure (PSI) at altitudes of	
Style of pack	Jar size	Process time	0–1,000 ft	Above 1,000 ft
Hot or Raw	Pints	25 min	10 lb	15 lb
	Quarts	30	10	15

CORN—WHOLE KERNEL

QUANTITY: About 4½ pounds of sweet corn in the husk are required to fill a quart jar with cut corn. You'll therefore need about 31½ pounds of sweet corn in the husk to fill 7 quart jars or about 20 pounds to fill 9 pint jars. A bushel of corn in the husk weighs 35 pounds and yields 6 to 11 quarts of cut corn.

QUALITY: Select ears of corn that are of ideal quality for eating fresh. Slightly less mature ears are fine, too, unless you are using an especially sweet variety. Very sweet corn varieties may turn brown in the jar if they are canned when they are too immature. You might want to try canning a small amount at first and checking the color and flavor before canning more.

PROCEDURE: Husk the corn, remove the silk, and wash the ears. Blanch them for 3 minutes in boiling water. Cut the corn from the cob at about ¾ the depth of the kernel. Do not scrape the cobs. If you're hot-packing, combine each quart of cut corn with 1 cup of hot water in a pot. Heat the corn to boiling, simmer 5 minutes, and ladle the hot corn and cooking liquid into hot pint or quart jars, leaving 1 inch headspace. If you're raw-packing, fill hot jars loosely with the raw corn, without pressing down on the corn or shaking the jars; leave 1 inch headspace. If you like, add ½ teaspoon of canning and pickling salt per pint to the jars. Then add freshly boiled water to cover the corn, maintaining the 1 inch headspace. Remove the air bubbles, and adjust the headspace if needed. Wipe the rims of the jars with a clean, dampened paper towel; apply the preheated lids and the screw bands; and process the jars in a pressure canner according to the tables that follow.

Whole-Kernel Corn						
Recommended process time in a dial-gauge pressure canner						
Style of pack	Jar size	Process time	Canner pressure (PSI) at altitudes of			
			0–2,000 ft	2,001–4,000 ft	4,001–6,000 ft	6,001–8,000 ft
Hot or Raw	Pints	55 min	11 lb	12 lb	13 lb	14 lb
	Quarts	85	11	12	13	14

Whole-Kernel Corn				
Recommended process time in a weighted-gauge pressure canner				
Style of pack	Jar size	Process time	Canner pressure (PSI) at altitudes of	
			0–1,000 ft	Above 1,000 ft
Hot or Raw	Pints	55 min	10 lb	15 lb
	Quarts	85	10	15

OKRA

QUANTITY: A quart jar holds about 1½ pounds of okra. You'll therefore need about 11 pounds of okra to fill 7 quart jars or about 7 pounds to fill 9 pint jars. A bushel of okra weighs 26 pounds and yields 16 to 18 quarts.

QUALITY: Select young, tender pods. Discard any that have rust spots or other signs of disease.

PROCEDURE: Wash the pods, and trim their stems. Leave pods whole, or cut them into 1-inch pieces. Put the okra into a pot, cover it with hot water, and bring the water to a boil. Boil the okra for 2 minutes. Fill hot pint or quart jars with the hot okra and cooking liquid, leaving 1 inch headspace. If you like, add ½ teaspoon of canning and pickling salt per pint to the jars. Remove the air bubbles, and adjust the headspace if needed. Wipe the rims of the jars with a clean, dampened paper towel; apply the preheated lids and the screw bands; and process the jars in a pressure canner according to the tables that follow.

Okra						
Recommended process time in a dial-gauge pressure canner						
			Canner pressure (PSI) at altitudes of			
Style of pack	Jar size	Process time	0–2,000 ft	2,001–4,000 ft	4,001–6,000 ft	6,001–8,000 ft
Hot	Pints	25 min	11 lb	12 lb	13 lb	14 lb
	Quarts	40	11	12	13	14

Okra				
Recommended process time in a weighted-gauge pressure canner				
			Canner pressure (PSI) at altitudes of	
Style of pack	Jar size	Process time	0–1,000 ft	Above 1,000 ft
Hot	Pints	25 min	10 lb	15 lb
	Quarts	40	10	15

PEAS, GREEN OR ENGLISH—SHELLED

This recipe is for shelled peas only. Peas in edible pods—that is, snap or snow peas—are best frozen rather than canned.

QUANTITY: About 4½ pounds of peas in the pod are required to fill a quart jar with shelled peas. You'll therefore need about 31½ pounds of peas in the pod to fill 7 quart jars with shelled peas or about 20 pounds to fill 9 pint jars. A bushel of peas in the pod weighs 30 pounds and yields 5 to 10 quarts of shelled peas.

QUALITY: Select pods filled with young, tender, sweet peas. Discard any pods that appear diseased.

PROCEDURE: Shell and rinse the peas. If you like, add ½ teaspoon of canning and pickling salt per pint to the hot jars. To hot-pack the peas, put them into a pot, cover them with boiling water, bring the water to a boil, and boil the peas for 2 minutes. Then fill the jars loosely with the hot peas and the cooking liquid, leaving 1 inch headspace. To raw-pack the peas, fill hot jars loosely with peas, without pressing down on the peas or shaking the jars; cover the peas with boiling water, leaving 1 inch headspace. Remove the air bubbles, and adjust the headspace if needed. Wipe the rims of the jars with a clean, dampened paper towel; apply the preheated lids and the screw bands; and process the jars in a pressure canner according to the tables that follow.

Green or English Peas						
Recommended process time in a dial-gauge pressure canner						
			Canner pressure (PSI) at altitudes of			
Style of pack	Jar size	Process time	0–2,000 ft	2,001–4,000 ft	4,001–6,000 ft	6,001–8,000 ft
Hot or Raw	Pints or Quarts	40 min	11 lb	12 lb	13 lb	14 lb

Green or English Peas				
Recommended process time in a weighted-gauge pressure canner				
			Canner pressure (PSI) at altitudes of	
Style of pack	Jar size	Process time	0–1,000 ft	Above 1,000 ft
Hot or Raw	Pints or Quarts	40 min	10 lb	15 lb

PEPPERS

For this recipe, peppers can be hot or sweet, green or ripe. Favorite varieties for canning include pimientos, Anaheims, and jalapeños.

QUANTITY: A pint jar holds about 1 pound of peppers. You'll therefore need about 9 pounds of peppers to fill 9 pint jars. A bushel of peppers weighs 25 pounds and yields 20 to 30 pints.

QUALITY: Select firm green, yellow, or red peppers. Do not use any that are soft or that show signs of disease.

Procedure: If you're using hot peppers, wear plastic or rubber gloves while handling them, and avoid touching your eyes or face. Leave small peppers whole; larger ones may be quartered. Cut 2 to 4 slits in each pepper. Either peel the peppers or blanch them in boiling water until they soften. To peel them, blister their skins in a hot oven (400°F) or under a broiler for 6 to 8 minutes or over a hot gas or electric burner covered with heavy wire mesh for several minutes; lay a damp cloth over the blistered peppers, and let them cool for several minutes before peeling off their skins. If you like, add ½ teaspoon canning and pickling salt per pint to the hot jars. Fill the jars loosely with the peeled or blanched peppers, flattening them if they're whole; leave 1 inch headspace. Add freshly boiled water to cover the peppers, keeping the 1 inch headspace. Remove the air bubbles, and adjust the headspace if needed. Wipe the rims of the jars with a clean, dampened paper towel; apply the preheated lids and the screw bands; and process the jars in a pressure canner according to the tables that follow.

Peppers
Recommended process time in a dial-gauge pressure canner

Style of pack	Jar size	Process time	Canner pressure (PSI) at altitudes of			
			0–2,000 ft	2,001–4,000 ft	4,001–6,000 ft	6,001–8,000 ft
Hot	Half-pints or Pints	35 min	11 lb	12 lb	13 lb	14 lb

Peppers
Recommended process time in a weighted-gauge pressure canner

Style of pack	Jar size	Process time	Canner pressure (PSI) at altitudes of	
			0–1,000 ft	Above 1,000 ft
Hot	Half-pints or Pints	35 min	10 lb	15 lb

POTATOES—CUBED OR WHOLE

QUANTITY: A quart jar holds 2½ to 3 pounds of small whole potatoes or cubed potatoes. You'll therefore need about 20 pounds of potatoes to fill 7 quart jars or about 13 pounds to fill 9 pint jars. A 50-pound bag of potatoes yields 18 to 22 quarts.

QUALITY: Select small- to medium-size mature potatoes of ideal quality for cooking. Avoid any that have been stored at a temperature below 45°F; chilling can cause discoloration when the potatoes are canned.

PROCEDURE. Wash and peel the potatoes. If they are no more than 2 inches in diameter, you can leave them whole. Otherwise, cut them into ½-inch cubes. Keep the cut potatoes in water containing ascorbic acid (see page 48) as you work. Then drain the potatoes, put them into a pot, cover them with boiling water, and bring the water to a boil. Cook the potatoes for 10 minutes if they're whole or 2 minutes if they're cubed, then drain them again. Bring fresh water to a boil. If you like, add ½ teaspoon of canning and pickling salt per pint to the hot jars. Fill the jars with the hot potatoes and hot water, leaving 1 inch headspace. Remove the air bubbles, and adjust the headspace if needed. Wipe the rims of the jars with a clean, dampened paper towel; apply the preheated lids and the screw bands; and process the jars in a pressure canner according to the tables that follow.

			Canner pressure (PSI) at altitudes of			
Style of pack	Jar size	Process time	0–2,000 ft	2,001–4,000 ft	4,001–6,000 ft	6,001–8,000 ft
Hot	Pints	35 min	11 lb	12 lb	13 lb	14 lb
	Quarts	40	11	12	13	14

Potatoes
Recommended process time in a dial-gauge pressure canner

Potatoes				
Recommended process time in a weighted-gauge pressure canner				
			Canner pressure (PSI) at altitudes of	
Style of pack	Jar size	Process time	0–1,000 ft	Above 1,000 ft
Hot	Pints	35 min	10 lb	15 lb
	Quarts	40	10	15

PUMPKIN OR WINTER SQUASH–CUBED

Don't can mashed or puréed pumpkin or squash. Can cubes instead, and drain and strain them when you're ready to make a pie or soup.

QUANTITY: About 2¼ pounds of whole pumpkin or winter squash, peeled and seeded and cut into cubes, will fill a quart jar. You'll therefore need 16 pounds of whole pumpkin or squash to fill 7 quart jars or about 10 pounds to fill 9 pint jars.

QUALITY: Pumpkins and winter squashes for canning should have hard rinds and stringless, mature pulp of ideal quality for cooking fresh. Small "sugar" or "pie" pumpkin varieties are better than big pumpkins for cooking and canning.

PROCEDURE: Wash and seed the pumpkins or squashes, cut them into 1-inch-wide slices, and peel the slices. Then cut the flesh into 1-inch cubes. Put the cubes into a pot, cover them with water, and boil them for 2 minutes. **Do not mash or purée the cubes.** Fill hot pint or quart jars with the cubes and cooking liquid, leaving 1 inch headspace. Remove the air bubbles, and adjust the headspace if needed. Wipe the rims of the jars with a clean, dampened paper towel; apply the preheated lids and the screw bands; and process the jars in a pressure canner according to the tables that follow.

Pumpkin or Winter Squash
Recommended process time in a dial-gauge pressure canner

Style of pack	Jar size	Process time	Canner pressure (PSI) at altitudes of			
			0–2,000 ft	2,001–4,000 ft	4,001–6,000 ft	6,001–8,000 ft
Hot	Pints	55 min	11 lb	12 lb	13 lb	14 lb
	Quarts	90	11	12	13	14

Pumpkin or Winter Squash
Recommended process time in a weighted-gauge pressure canner

Style of pack	Jar size	Process time	Canner pressure (PSI) at altitudes of	
			0–1,000 ft	Above 1,000 ft
Hot	Pints	55 min	10 lb	15 lb
	Quarts	90	10	15

SQUASH, WINTER—CUBED

Prepare and process winter squash according to the instructions for "Pumpkin or Winter Squash—Cubed," on the previous page.

SWEET POTATOES—PIECES OR WHOLE

QUANTITY: A quart jar holds about 2½ pounds of sweet potatoes. You'll therefore need about 17½ pounds of sweet potatoes to fill 7 quart jars or about 11 pounds to fill 9 pint jars. A bushel of sweet potatoes weighs 50 pounds and yields 17 to 25 quarts.

QUALITY: Choose small to medium sweet potatoes that are mature but not too fibrous. Can them within 2 months after harvest.

PROCEDURE: Wash the sweet potatoes, and boil or steam them until they are partially soft, 15 to 20 minutes. Remove skins. Cut larger sweet potatoes into pieces of uniform size; leave small sweet potatoes whole. **Don't mash or purée sweet potatoes before canning.** Pack the sweet potatoes into hot pint or quart jars, leaving 1 inch headspace. If you like, add ½ teaspoon of canning and pickling salt per pint to the jars. Cover the sweet potatoes with freshly boiled water, but keep the 1 inch headspace. Remove the air bubbles, and adjust the headspace if needed. Wipe the rims of the jars with a clean, dampened paper towel; apply the preheated lids and the screw bands; and process the jars in a pressure canner according to the tables that follow.

Sweet Potatoes Recommended process time in a dial-gauge pressure canner						
Style of pack	Jar size	Process time	Canner pressure (PSI) at altitudes of			
			0–2,000 ft	2,001–4,000 ft	4,001–6,000 ft	6,001–8,000 ft
Hot	Pints	65 min	11 lb	12 lb	13 lb	14 lb
	Quarts	90	11	12	13	14

Sweet Potatoes Recommended process time in a weighted-gauge pressure canner				
Style of pack	Jar size	Process time	Canner pressure (PSI) at altitudes of	
			0–1,000 ft	Above 1,000 ft
Hot	Pints	65 min	10 lb	15 lb
	Quarts	90	10	15